Studies in Jewish Jurisprudence
Vol. V

DIVORCE
IN
JEWISH LAW AND LIFE

Studies in Jewish Jurisprudence

Vol. V

DIVORCE IN JEWISH LAW AND LIFE

By Irwin H. Haut

SEPHER-HERMON PRESS
New York

DIVORCE
IN
JEWISH LAW AND LIFE

By
Irwin H. Haut

SEPHER-HERMON PRESS
New York

DIVORCE IN JEWISH LAW AND LIFE
Copyright © 1983 Irwin H. Haut
Published by:
Sepher-Hermon Press, Inc.
ISBN 0-87203-110-1 (hardcover)
ISBN 0-87203-114-4 (paper)

Library of Congress Cataloging in Publication Data

Haut, Irwin H.
    Divorce in Jewish law and life.

    (Studies in Jewish jurisprudence ; 5)
    Bibliography: p.
    1. Divorce (Jewish law)   I. Title.   II. Series.
LAW   296.1'8   83-12671
ISBN 0-87203-110-1

לרבקה

CONTENTS

INTRODUCTION

The rising divorce rate in the secular society has impacted upon the Jewish community, resulting in recent years in an increasing number of individuals who seek redress in the civil courts for problems encountered by the inability of either spouse to attain the religious termination of a marriage by the "giving" or "accepting" of a Jewish divorce, a "get," upon the civil termination of their marriage. From the decisions of the courts, as well as other indications to date, it appears that the courts, the attorneys, and the public at large are unaware of the intricacies of Jewish law in this area. Thus, the primary function of this work is to provide some essential background for all concerned, regarding the basic nature of the Jewish laws of marriage and divorce.

I have not attempted an exhaustive presentation of the entire vast and variegated corpus of Jewish law in these areas. I have, however, in Part I of this work, attempted to set forth and explain those areas of Jewish laws of marriage and divorce that are pertinent to a fuller understanding of the nature of the "get," including its necessity, function, limitations, procedure and other topics, which are most relevant to modern conditions and to the problems arising in divorce litigation.

Part I of this work is essentially devoted to a discussion of principles of Jewish laws of marriage and divorce as presented in the Bible, particularly in the Torah (Pentateuch), and in the Talmud. I will also discuss the views of the Rabbis of the Mishnaic period, known as "Tannaim." This period is terminated with the codification of the Mishna, a collection of Jewish law prepared and edited by Rabbi Yehuda HaNasi, in approximately 220 C.E. I shall also present the views of the successors of the Tannaim, the "Amoraim," Rabbis who flourished between 220 C.E and 503 C.E., whose views are recorded in the Babylonian Talmud, which was completed at approximately the latter date. I hope that this will afford an adequate foundation for an understanding of Jewish law for present-day purposes.

In order to comprehend modern developments regarding enforcement in the secular courts of agreements to "give" or "accept" a get, I have devoted portions of Part I to a discussion of the Jewish marriage contract, the "ketubah," as well as to a discussion of a get given under compulsion. In addition, and in order to place the role of the Rabbis in proper perspective, I have included a chapter on Rabbinic legislative power and authority.

In Part II, I have traced the development of Jewish divorce law from the end of the Talmudic era through the Middle Ages, with a discussion of the decrees and enactments of the Geonim, Rabbis who flourished in Babylonia from approximately 600 C.E. to 1100 C.E., as well as of other giants of Jewish law, including Maimonides (1135–1204 C.E.) and Rabbenu Gershom (960–1028 C.E.).

The common denominator of this period of Jewish law is an attempt by the Rabbis to impart a measure of equality with regard to the obtaining of a get by the wife, or, as in the case of Rabbenu Gershom, to afford a measure of protection for the wife with regard to get. Parts I and II are, therefore, essentially a necessary prelude for a fuller understanding of the modern conditions and problems arising in divorce and get litigation, to which the remainder of this work is devoted.

In Part III, I discuss Jewish divorce in modern times, with the arrival upon the historic scene of secular (or civil) divorce, with its attendant complications for Jewish law, as well as various responses of Jewish law thereto, including the modification of the traditional ketubah that has been adopted by the Conservative branch of American Judaism. I also provide a review of the relevant cases decided in New York State and elsewhere, as well as in Israel, and of the status of court enforcement or involvement with the "giving" or "acceptance" of a get.

In Part IV, I discuss future prospects for the resolution of the problem of the "agunah," the "anchored wife" who is unable to remarry, being unable to "obtain" a get. I present several Rabbinic suggestions now under consideration, as well as my own proposal for a viable solution to this problem.

It is hoped that this work will aid the courts, the Matrimonial Bar, and the general public to attain a better and deeper understanding of Jewish law in these relevant areas. It is also hoped that this work will provide a basis for further discussion amongst Rabbinic circles regarding resolutions of this problem, and will be a spur to the same, whether or not future solutions will be similar to those presented by me. It is imperative that a viable resolution of this problem be arrived at, a goal towards which this work is directed.

This work had its genesis in 1959, when, fresh out of Yeshiva University, I was surprised to be confronted with the legal problems arising from the use of the Conservative Ketubah in a course in Family Law, taught by Professor Caleb Foote, at the University of Pennsylvania Law School.

On the same faculty were my mentors and friends, Professors A. Leo Levin and Louis Henkin, both also of Yeshiva University, and Professor John Honnold, who aided and abetted what was to become for me a life-long fascination with the intricacies of common law, as well as its relationship to Jewish law (*Mishpat Ivri*), particularly in the areas of marriage and divorce, and commercial law, in which areas I have since had occasion to write.

Over the years, my interest in Divorce Law has grown, due both to my involvement with various organizations whose purpose is to deal with the problems arising from divorce litigation, and with my frequent contacts with those unfortunate individuals embroiled therein.

I would like to acknowledge my indebtedness to David Werner Amram's book *Jewish Law of Divorce*, a pioneering work in this area, which was relied upon by me, particularly with regard to the organization of Part I of this work, and, specifically, chapter VI, dealing with the formal requirements of a get. This work, despite its many errors and deficiencies, constituted a most worthwhile and first attempt at presentation in the English language of the entire scope of Jewish law of divorce, by a noted and respected legal scholar.

I would also like to express my sincerest thanks to my colleague and fellow attorney, Rabbi Judah Dick Esq., for reading the manuscript of this work, and for his learned suggestions, as well as to Mr. Samuel Gross of Sepher-Hermon Press, for initiating this project and for his very constructive and helpful collaboration in this work since its inception.

Lastly, I wish to express my thanks to my wife Rivkah, and to my daughters, Sheryl and Tamara, for being patient with me for the time consumed in writing this book. May they and all Jewish daughters be henceforth spared the problems that are discussed in this book.

May the Almighty look with favor upon His people, and impart to its leaders the wisdom necessary to resolve the problems existing in this troubled area of Jewish law.

Brooklyn, New York
March 1983   Irwin H. Haut

Part I
THE LAW

Chapter I
MARRIAGE AND
ITS OBLIGATIONS

Any discussion of Jewish Law of Divorce must begin with a discussion of Jewish Law of Marriage, and of marital obligations as well. Under Jewish law, marriage is essentially a contractual arrangement solemnized by a religious ceremony. The marriage and marital status are effectuated by a symbolic act of "kinyan," or acquisition.

Thus, by analogy to civil acts of *kinyan* or acquisition generally, the presentation by the groom to the bride of an item of monetary value (usually a ring), of nominal worth,[1] and the voluntary acceptance of that item by the bride, is sufficient to effectuate marriage, or "kiddushin."[2]

It should be clearly understood that the utilization of the civil concept of *kinyan* in connection with marriage is one by analogy only, and there should be no implication that marriage is thereby compared to commercial transactions generally. Thus, as noted by one authority, it is only when reference to marriage was made in the Talmud in connection with rules relating to acquisition generally that the term "kinyan" was utilized. But, when marriage in the usual sense is being referred to, the generic term "kiddushin" (lit. consecration) is properly used.[3]

Under Biblical and Talmudic law, the aspect of the marital relationship which is most clearly defined by the term "kiddushin" is that of the consecration of the bride to her husband, with no permissibility of sexual relations with any other male for the duration of the marriage.[4] However, polygamy was also permitted, being prohibited only in comparatively recent times by a decree (*takanah*) of Rabbenu Gershom,[5] which will be discussed more fully below.

As noted previously, the marital state, or *kiddushin*, is effected by the presentation of an item of nominal value to the bride by the groom. This ritual must be accompanied by various other formal requirements, including the presence of two competent witnesses, and the following formal declaration by the groom:

> You are hereby wedded to me with this ring according to the laws of Moses and Israel.[6]

Under classical Jewish law, *kiddushin* could also be effected by two other means, both of which have gradually become obsolete. *Kiddushin* can also be solemnized by a formal writ or note (*shtar*), presented by the groom to the bride, or by sexual relations.[7] However, over the course of time, and particularly because the latter manner of effecting *kiddushin* was frowned upon by the Rabbis, the method prevailing in the present is that of giving a ring, or other item of nominal value. Nevertheless, the cohabitation mode of formalizing *kiddushin* is a basis for the presumption that a man does not have sexual relations with a woman merely for the sake of promiscuity, and also for various other rules founded on that presumption,[8] some of which will be discussed, where relevant, in the course of this book.

A further clarification is in order for a better comprehension of marriage under Jewish law. In earlier times, Jewish law carefully distinguished between "eirusin," commonly but erroneously translated as betrothal or engagement, and "nisuin," or consummation of the marriage. Thus, technically, the giving and acceptance of an item of value, by the groom and bride respectively (or, in earlier days, by formal writ, or *shtar*, or by cohabitation, referred to above) created a status between the parties of "eirusin." This state was more than a mere betrothal or engagement, as it did indeed constitute the marital state itself, with a very limited but significant exception—the right of cohabitation. In other words, the parties were indeed wedded to each other, but the bride remained in her parents' home for a period of time, usually one year. Thereafter, she moved to her husband's home where the marriage was consummated. The commencement of family life in the newlyweds' own home was termed "nisuin."

In relatively recent times, the acts constituting *eirusin* and *nisuin* have been consolidated into the marriage ceremony as we know it. *Eirusin* is effected by the giving and acceptance of an item of value by the groom and bride respectively, accompanied by the ritual requirements referred to above. *Nisuin* is effected by the bride and groom secluding themselves thereafter for a short period of time in a private room adjacent to the area where the *erusin* had taken place.[9] Thus, the modern Jewish marriage ceremony is really a combination of these two separate acts.

The marital relationship, once entered into, carries with it a host of reciprocal duties between husband and wife, including, of course, mutual love, affection and respect.[10] The obligations of a husband to his wife are as follows:[11]

to provide food for her,
to provide clothing for her,
to engage in periodic sexual relations with her,
to provide her with a ketubah,[12]
to provide medicine and medical treatment for her if
necessary,
to ransom her if she is taken captive,
to provide for her burial.

As part of her marital rights, the wife, if widowed, has, among others, the right to be supported from her husband's estate, and to reside in the marital abode until her death or her remarriage.[13]

The husband, on the other hand, has rights to the following:

his wife's earnings, during the subsistence of the
marriage,
property found by his wife,
the produce of property owned by his wife prior to the
marriage,
inheritance of his wife's property upon her death.[14]

A marriage entered into under Jewish law is terminated only by the death of either spouse, or by the giving and acceptance of a "get" (the Rabbinic term for a writ of divorce, plural "gittin").[15]

Chapter II
THE KETUBAH

The "ketubah" is a document that is presented by the groom to the bride, and which embodies the obligations undertaken by the husband, which are, for the most part, imposed upon him by law.

Under the terms of the ketubah, the husband initially declares himself obligated to provide for his wife's physical needs. In addition, he accepts certain monetary obligations, the purpose of which is to render divorce more difficult. As will be discussed more fully in chapter IV, under Jewish law only the husband can give a get, and, according to Biblical and Talmudic law, this get may be given against the will of the wife, although this latter rule has been abrogated in post-Talmudic times.[1] Therefore, if not for the monetary burdens in the event of a divorce, which are explicitly provided for in the ketubah, it would be easy indeed for a man to dissolve the bonds of marriage by the simple expedient of serving his wife with a get.[2] These monetary obligations, therefore, acted as a check or restraint upon the husband in the event of a hasty decision to divorce his wife.

The wife may not waive her right to the ketubah, nor may she continue to cohabit with her husband if the ketubah is lost or destroyed until another one is written.[3]

Under the present terms of the ketubah, the husband obligates himself (by *kinyan*) in the following manner:

> to pay his wife in the event of divorce, or upon his death (payable from his estate), 200 zuz in the case of a woman who was never previously married, and 100 zuz in the case of one who was. This is known as the "Basic Ketubah,"
>
> to pay to his wife an additional sum, known as "Ketubah Increment" (this is voluntary),
>
> to return to his wife, upon dissolution of the marriage, any property brought by her into the marriage. Since the husband is permitted to trade with this property during the term of the marriage, it is the custom for him to pay an additional amount over and above the amount of property actually brought into the marriage by the wife, representing the profit realized by the husband during the course of his handling of the property.

Today, it is generally the custom to consolidate all such sums under the general statement of 200 zuz and 100 zuz, in cases of previously unmarried and married women respectively. However, if the wife can prove that specific and greater amounts are due her with respect to the last item above, such is permitted.[4]

The text of the Ketubah is as follows:[5]

> On the　　　　day of　　　　, thus did　　　　, son of　　　　, say to　　　　, daughter of　　　　, never married bride: 'Be unto me for a wife, according to the laws of Moses and Israel, and I will work, honor, support and maintain thee in accordance with the manner of Jewish men who work, honor, support and maintain their wives in faithfulness and I give thee bride price of　　　　zuz　　　　which are due thee　　　　and thy food, clothing

and needs, and shall come to thee according to the way of all the earth.' And ⸏⸏⸏⸏ consented and has become his wife. And this is the dowry that she has brought from the house of ⸏⸏⸏⸏ in silver, gold, ornaments, articles of wear, utensils of dwelling, bedclothes; all has this bridegroom ⸏⸏⸏⸏ taken upon himself in ⸏⸏⸏⸏ refined pure silver, and this bridegroom has consented and added to it from his own another ⸏⸏⸏⸏ refined, pure silver corresponding to this, the sum total being ⸏⸏⸏⸏ refined, pure silver. And thus did ⸏⸏⸏⸏ this bridegroom say: 'The responsibility of this ketubah, this dowry and this addition I take upon myself and on my heirs after me, to pay from all the best, desirable property and acquisitions that I have under all the heaven which I acquired or which I shall acquire in the future, property which has a guarantee or which does not have a guarantee, all shall be guaranteed and assured to pay from them this ketubah, this dowry and this addition, from me and even from the cloak on my shoulder, in my lifetime or after my death, from this day on, forever!' The guarantee and severity of this ketubah, this dowry and this addition, has ⸏⸏⸏⸏ this bridegroom taken upon himself as the severity of all the documents of ketubah and additions which are customary for the daughters of Israel, which are made according to the ordinances of our sages, their memory be a blessing.

The ketubah, by its express language, is a lien and a prior claim on the husband's estate with respect to all property owned by him during his lifetime,[6] and, in the event of his death or divorce, is paid out of the "best" and "desirable" portions thereof.[7]

As stated previously,[8] marriage is effectuated in Jewish law through an act of *kinyan*. The obligations set forth in the ketubah, too, are undertaken by the husband through an act of *kinyan*. This is accomplished prior to the wedding ceremony, when the groom and bride each lifts a handkerchief, proffered by the rabbi performing the ceremony. By this symbolic act of *kinyan*, the husband presently assumes the specific monetary obligations set forth in the ketubah.[9]

Although the purpose of the ketubah is essentially the protection of the wife, the wife may, by misconduct, forfeit her right to all or some portions of it. In this regard, it must be noted that the wife *never* loses her right to the return of that portion of her property which she brought into the marriage.[10] Thus, the forfeiture aspects of a wife's misconduct apply only to the "Main Ketubah" and "Ketubah Increment" referred to above.[11]

The instances when a wife forfeits her rights to such portions of the ketubah are subsumed under the term "moredet" (rebellious wife). In those instances the husband could, under classical Jewish law (which permitted divorce against the will of the wife) divorce his wife without incurring any obligations as set out in the ketubah.[12] In the following instances, among others, the wife's right to the ketubah is forfeited:

> 1   where she violated the "Mosaic and Jewish law" as, for example, if she served her husband food that had not been tithed, or food otherwise forbidden, or if she had sexual relations with her husband whilst she was menstruating, without informing him of this;[13]
> 2   where she violated conventional morality as, for example, if she appeared in public bare-headed, or with her hair loose, or if she flirted with strangers.[14]

Similar rules also apply in cases of the wife's unfaithfulness,[15] or if she had physical defects which she had concealed from her husband, including the inability to bear children. This applies only when the wife was aware of these defects before the marriage, and the husband was not, and he could not, by due diligence, have ascertained their existence.[16]

A further category of *moredet* is that of the rebellious wife who refuses to engage in sexual relations with her husband. Because of the intrinsic importance of this area of law in connection with attempts by the Rabbis to equalize the status of the spouses in divorce litigation, this subject will be discussed separately below.[17]

Chapter III
RABBINIC LEGISLATION
("TAKANAH") IN AREAS OF
MARRIAGE AND DIVORCE

The creative and progressive role of the Rabbis in the growth and development of Jewish law has oft been overlooked by both layman and scholar alike. In speaking of the judges and of their role in an ordered society, the Torah states (Deut. 17:11):

> You shall act in accordance with the instructions given you and the ruling handed down to you; you must not deviate from the judgement that they announce to you either to the right or to the left.

In the course of time, the courts, and particularly the Highest Court (the Sanhedrin), were vested with legislative and administrative authority, in addition to their usual judicial function.[1] The exercise of this legislative function by the Rabbis resulted in enactments known as "takanot" (sing. "takanah"),[2] enjoying the force of law.

Although the Rabbis were vested with such legislative or rule-making authority in all areas of Jewish law, civil, criminal, and ritual-religious, for our present purpose it is necessary to discuss only the most pervasive nature of their authority in the areas of marriage and divorce.

As mentioned previously, both the marriage formula and the ketubah proclaim that they are being entered into or undertaken "according to the laws of Moses and Israel." This has resulted in the concept that "all who marry are presumed to do so in consonance with the will of the Rabbis."[3] It follows, therefore, that when an act of an individual runs contrary to the will of the Rabbis, as expressed by a takanah in the area of marriage and divorce, then they are thereby empowered to take whatever remedial action is necessary, including retroactive annulment of the marriage, in order to protect the public interest sought to be served by the takanah.[4]

One example from the Talmud suffices to graphically illustrate the rule-making authority of the Rabbis to retroactively annul a valid marriage by a takanah. In the Mishna, *Gittin*, 4:1, various rules are set forth regarding one who sends a get to his wife, and thereafter, and before the agent physically delivers the get, declares that the agency is revoked. It is clear that under Torah law the husband is fully authorized to do so. The marriage, therefore, continues to remain in force. However, the dangers inherent in this approach are quite obvious, for, if the husband is permitted to do so, the agent, unaware of the fact that the agency was revoked, would still deliver the get, and the woman would consider herself permitted to remarry, when in law, and in fact, she is still married.

The Mishna states:

> If one sent a get to his wife (by an agent) and he overtook the agent (prior to actual delivery of the get) . . . and he revoked the agency, the agency stands revoked . . . However, once the get was delivered, the agency can no longer be revoked. In earlier times, one was permitted to revoke the agency (before delivery of the get) before a

court (beth din, i.e., not in the presence of the agent). But then Rabban Gamliel the Elder decreed (enacted a takanah) that such may not be done as a matter of public policy.

The Talmud then presents a dispute between Rabbi Yehuda Hanasi and Rabbi Shimon ben Gamliel (son of Rabban Gamliel the Elder, quoted in the Mishna) as to the legal effect of the husband's act of revoking the agency in violation of the takanah of Rabban Gamliel the Elder.[5]

Thus, when, despite the takanah, the husband has attempted to revoke the agency outside of the agent's presence, the view of Rabbi Yehuda is that it stands revoked, as under Torah law, and the wife is not permitted to remarry. Rabbi Shimon's view, however, is that the husband no longer has any power to revoke the agency, since that act is in violation of the takanah, and to permit a husband to violate the takanah with impunity would render nugatory the exercise of the court's power.[6]

It is thus quite apparent that, under the view of Rabbi Shimon, subsequently concurred in by Rabbi Yehuda,[7] the takanah in question can invalidate or annul a marriage that remains valid under Torah law. The Talmud then proceeds to analyze the sources for such Rabbinic authority to indeed overrule the Torah itself, as follows:[8]

And how is it, that under Torah law, the get is invalid (the agency to deliver it having been revoked) and because of this (the takanah of Rabban Gamliel the Elder) we permit a married woman to remarry? Yes, this is the correct rule, for all who marry (are presumed to) do so in accordance with the will of the Rabbis, and the Rabbis have (in the exercise of their legislative authority) annuled this marriage (retroactively).

The foregoing reflects quite conclusively the wide-ranging powers of the Rabbis to retroactively annul an otherwise valid marriage. We will continually return to this theme and concept.

Chapter IV
THE JEWISH DIVORCE

A halachically valid marriage can be terminated only in two ways: either by the death of a spouse, or by the giving of a get. Although a brief reference to the manner of terminating a marriage by get is found in the Torah,[1] the Talmudic literature is replete with rules relating to divorce. Indeed, there is an entire tractate of the Talmud devoted to this subject, Tractate Gittin.

The text of a get is as follows:[2]

> On the   day of the week, the   day of the month of   , in the year   from the creation of the world according to the calendar reckoning we are accustomed to count here in the city   (which is also known as   ) which is located on the river   (and on the river   ) and situated near wells of water, I   (also known as   ) the son of   (also known as   ) who today am present in the city   (which is also known as   ) which is located on the river   (and on the river   ) and situated near wells of water, do willingly consent, being under no restraint, to release, to set free and put aside thee, my wife   (also known as   ) daughter of   (also known as   ) who is today in the city of

(which is also known as   ) which is located on the
river   (and on the river   ) and situated near
wells of water, who has been my wife from before. Thus, I
do set free, release thee, and put thee aside, in order that
thou may have permission and the authority over thyself
to go and marry any man thou may desire. No person may
hinder thee from this day onward, and thou art permitted
to every man. This shall be for thee from me a bill of
dismissal, a letter of release, and a document of freedom,
in accordance with the laws of Moses and Israel.

> .... the son of ...., witness
> .... the son of ...., witness

It is a fundamental principle in Jewish law that only a
husband can give a get. The function of a wife is limited to
merely being the recipient of a get.[3]

A corollary of this rule, under classical Jewish law, is that
the giving of a get can be effectuated even against the will of
a wife.[4] The Talmud states: "A wife is divorced either will-
ingly or unwillingly, but a husband divorces only from his
own free will."[5]

TORAITIC LIMITATIONS UPON
A HUSBAND'S RIGHT TO DIVORCE

The absolute right on the part of a husband to divorce his
wife is limited under the Torah to only two instances: that of
a man who rapes an unmarried woman,[6] and that of a newly
married groom who falsely accuses his bride of having had
sexual experience with a stranger after *eirusin*.[7] In the former
instance, the rapist is directed to marry his victim if she
consents, and is prohibited from ever divorcing her. He must
also pay to her father the sum of 50 shekalim. In the latter
instance, that of the husband who falsely accused his wife,

he is similarly enjoined from ever divorcing her. In this case, he must also pay to her father the sum of 100 shekalim.

TALMUDIC LIMITATIONS UPON A HUSBAND'S RIGHT TO DIVORCE

There was a sharp difference of opinion amongst the Rabbis regarding valid grounds for divorce. The School of Shammai[8] was of the opinion that divorce is permitted only when a wife commits adultery.[9] The School of Hillel[10] held that a husband's right to divorce is limited to instances in which some cause, however slight or minimal, exists, as, for example, if a husband wishes to divorce his wife because she burnt his food.[11] Rabbi Akiva [12] held the extreme view that a husband can divorce his wife even if she gives him no cause whatsoever, as, for example, if he sets his eyes on another woman.[13]

The view that became accepted is that of the School of Hillel, and, although divorce for frivolous or slight grounds is frowned upon, especially with respect to a first marriage,[14] it is permitted.

It thus appears that, under classical Jewish law, a husband's absolute right to divorce is almost unlimited, except for the above mentioned cases. Furthermore, divorce was required to be the result of the free exercise of a husband's will. And yet the Rabbis developed a theory whereby they forced a recalcitrant husband to give a get, against his will as it were, in various circumstances. This was accomplished through the use of a legal fiction. It was an early established rule that, where appropriate and permitted by Jewish law, the Jewish courts could exercise duress or coercion upon a husband, through incarceration, corporal punishment, or other means, until he gives his formal consent to the get.[15] However, if, despite such coercion, the husband still stubbornly refuses to give a get, there is little, if anything, that can be done.[16]

This situation is a result of the essential nature of the get. Unlike the situation prevailing in other societies and legal systems, the giving of a get (as well as the entering into a marriage) is a personal act between husband and wife, with the courts (or, indeed, the state, as in Israel today) playing or taking no role insofar as the actual effectuation of the divorce is concerned.[17] In certain instances, to which we shall return, and in appropriate circumstances, the aid of the Jewish courts is invoked, in order to coerce the husband into giving a get. But, the role of the courts, even in such circumstances, is that of aiding the enforcement of rights otherwise existing under Jewish law. However, under legal theory, it is the husband, and he alone, who gives a get, and neither the courts nor the state.[18]

A husband is furthermore limited in his right to give a get under a variety of circumstances. Thus, if a wife is insane, or mentally incompetent, to the extent that she cannot care for her own safety, she may not be divorced.[19] However, if she is rational enough to perceive that she is divorced, to the extent that she will not return to her former husband, then she may be divorced.[20] Because of similar reasons it was held that a minor wife, one who is so young as to be unable to care for herself, and to understand the nature of the get, may not be divorced, if her father, to whose care she would normally return, is deceased.[21]

In addition to these limitations upon the husband's theoretical ability to divorce his wife with ease, there are also extensive formalities attendant upon the writing of a get, which we will discuss more fully below,[22] as well as the monetary ketubah obligations affected by the get. These factors serve as a deterrent and check upon hasty and ill-advised divorce, although, strictly speaking, they do not constitute an actual limitation on the husband's right to divorce.

We see, therefore, that the seemingly absolute right of the husband to divorce his wife was frequently limited by the Rabbis, as they saw fit, and where demanded by the circumstances.

It follows from the foregoing that Jewish law, unlike the situation prevailing in Western societies,[23] permits divorce by consent of the parties. This right of the parties to no-fault divorce is directly related to and arises from the concept that divorce is essentially a matter of personal contract between the parties, and, as such, is dependent on their will for its implementation.[24]

Chapter V
A WIFE'S RIGHT
TO SUE FOR DIVORCE

A wife's right to sue for divorce, under Jewish law, is predicated upon a legal fiction. As we noted previously,[1] divorce is effectuated only through the free exercise of a husband's will. And yet, when the Talmudic Sages felt that in law and in justice a husband must give his wife a get, they permitted the use of force and other means of coercion to be applied until the husband gave his consent to the get. A get so given is not deemed as being one given under duress and hence invalid, but is deemed valid by the Rabbis, so long as the husband formally assents.

Maimonides' view in this regard is both novel and interesting. His rationale for permitting the use of such legal fiction, which is in itself quite radical, is that essentially the husband really does intend to act in accordance with Jewish law. Since that law, as articulated by the Rabbis, declares that he must give his wife a get, it is hence his obligation to do so. His refusal to give a get, however, is the result of an evil disposition, that prompts him to act contrary to law. Therefore, reasons Maimonides, since it is only his evil disposition which prevents him from following the directives of the Rabbis, duress may be applied to weaken or to drive away his evil inclination, with the result being that when he finally gives his consent, *he does so from his own free will.*[2]

In any event, and whether or not one agrees with this subjective rationale for the "legal fiction" involved, it is an incontrovertible fact that the legal fiction of "constructive consent" has proven to be of inestimable value in Jewish law, and is applicable in all circumstances where the husband is obligated to give a get (e.g., if he has a loathsome disease, and is therefore repulsive to his wife).

A crucial limitation on the application of this rule is that the court which applies such coercion be a duly constituted court (Beth Din).[3] If, however, the get was not so required under Jewish law (e.g., the wife has no valid basis for her desire for the divorce), it is not valid, as it constitutes a get given under duress.[4]

Similarly, if a Gentile court (or, indeed, if individual Jews and not a Beth Din) forced a husband to give a get, it is invalid, being considered a get given under duress, even if it was otherwise required under Jewish law. However, it is a subject of dispute whether such invalidity is Toraitic or Rabbinic in nature.[5] Yet, if a Gentile court (or either Gentiles or Jews acting individually) merely compelled a husband to follow and obey the directives of a Jewish court, which had previously directed him to give a get, the get so given is generally held to be valid, although there is some minority opinion[6] to the contrary.

These principles have had extensive application, with regard to attempts in both earlier times as well as today, to enlist the aid of Gentiles, or of Gentile courts, to resolve the problem of a husband who refuses to give his wife a get. This situation will be discussed more fully below.[7]

A wife has the right to sue for divorce in the following circumstances:

1. If her husband becomes afflicted with a loathsome disease after marriage, or if the existence of the disease was unknown to her prior to the marriage.[8]
2. If her husband is impotent or sterile.[9]
3. If her husband refuses to provide her with necessaries, or refuses to engage in sexual relations with her.[10]
4. If she is subjected to physical or verbal abuse by her husband,[11] or to misconduct, as, for example, if he forces her to violate a religious precept.[12]
5. If her husband is engaged in some malodorous occupation, such as gathering dog's dung, smelting copper, or tanning hides.[13]
6. If her husband seeks to leave the place where the couple resides, and to move to another country, he can be compelled to give her a get if she refuses to go with him.[14]
7. If her husband becomes an apostate. In this case it is deemed lawful to appeal to the Gentile courts to force the apostate to give a get.[15]

The foregoing is not intended to be an exhaustive presentation of the instances wherein a wife may sue for divorce under classical Jewish law. It serves, however, as exemplary of the lengths to which the Talmudic Rabbis went to afford some measure of protection to the wife in the instance of an ill-advised marriage.

בשני בשבת בששה ימים לירח אלול שנת חמשת אלפים ושש מאות וחמשים

וחמש לבריאת עולם למנינא דרגילנא למימן ביה הכא במתא פילאדעלפיא

איך אנא שמואל בן משה דממתא ווילנא וכל שום אחרן וחניכה דאית לי ולאבהתי

ולאתרי ולאתריהון דאבהתי צביתי ברעוא נפשי בדלא אניסנא ופטרית ושבקית

ותרוכית יתיכי ליכי אנת רחל בת יוסף דממתא זיטאמיר וכל שום אחרן וחניכה

דאית ליכי ולאבהתיכי ולאתריכי ולאתריהון דאבהתיכי די הוית אנתתי מן קדמת

דנא וכדו פטרית ושבקית ותרוכית יתיכי ליכי די תהוייין

רשאה ושלטאה בנפשיכי לכל

להתנסבא לכל גבר דיתצבייין ואיש לא ימחא

בידיכי מן יומא דנן ולעלם והרי את מותרת לכל איש

ודן די יהוי ליכי מנאי ספר תרוכין וגט פטורין ואגרת שבוקין

כדת משה וישראל

יהודה בן בנימין הכהן עד
אהרן בן אפרים עד

A GET OR BILL OF DIVORCE.

Chapter VI
FORMAL REQUIREMENTS OF GET

The formal requirements of a get are many and varied, and may have been enacted to serve as a check against a hasty and ill-advised decision by a husband to divorce his wife.

Among the formal, technical requirements are the following:[1]

1. *Date*. The get must be dated and, according to the usually prevailing custom, it is dated from the year of creation of the world (i.e., 1983 C.E.=5,743). If the date was erroneous or omitted, it is not valid.[2]

2. *Names of the Parties*. It is well established that a get must be written for particularly specified individuals. Thus, the husband must specifically request that the get be written for his wife, and the exact names of the parties must be included therein by the scribe preparing the get. In addition, any nicknames by which the parties are known must also be inserted in the get.[3]

3. *Residence of the Parties*. The place of residence of the parties must be set forth.[4]

4. *Words of Separation*. Since the get certifies divorce, and establishes the termination of the marital relationship, it is necessary to have words of complete separation set forth

in it. It must therefore be explicitly stated that the wife is henceforth permitted to remarry at her will.[5]

If a husband attempts to limit the get by stating in it that "You are permitted to marry anyone except X," he causes the get to be invalid, because it does not effect a total separation of the parties.[6] The husband is, however, permitted to attach conditions to the validity of the get, as, for example, "You are divorced on condition that you pay me 100 zuz." If the condition was not fulfilled, the get is rendered invalid.[7]

If a husband did not attempt to limit his wife's right to remarry in connection with the get by stating "You are permitted to marry anyone except X" but instead he merely attached a condition to the get, that it was given "On condition that you do not marry X," some authorities hold that such is a valid get. They reason that this condition is no different than any other type of condition that a husband can attach to the get.[8] Other authorities, however, hold that such condition effectively restricts the wife's right to remarry, and hence prevents the complete cutting off and termination of the marital relationship. Under these latter views, the condition is unenforceable, and the divorce is invalid.[9]

The concept of a "conditional get" was often utilized in circumstances wherein it was sought to prevent a wife from experiencing difficulties in case of the death or disappearance of her husband. In the former instance, the death of the husband, without his having previously divorced his wife, might result in her being required to undergo a "ḥalitzah" ceremony. This ceremony is necessary under Biblical[10] and Rabbinic[11] law if a husband dies childless and leaves a surviving brother. In these circumstances, the brother is obligated to take his deceased brother's widow to be his wife. This is called "Yibbum." If he refuses to do so, he may avoid this *Yibbum* obligation by participating in a ceremony known as "ḥalitzah." (Without the *ḥalitzah* ceremony, the widow is prohibited from marrying a third party.) To avoid the invocation of these rules, if, for example, a husband was seriously ill, he would give his wife a get which would, prior to his death, become retroactively effective to the time when it was given.[12]

Another application of these principles is in circumstances wherein a husband was embarking upon a dangerous voyage or journey, or was going off to war. It was similarly sought in order to prevent the wife's becoming an "agunah" in case of the husband's disappearance.

Under Jewish law, unlike common law, there exists no presumption of death from absence. If a husband disappeared, his wife may not remarry in absence of evidence satisfactory to the court of her husband's death. A woman so unable to remarry is termed an "agunah" (lit., anchored woman). In order to prevent this problem, the Rabbis utilized a get-on-condition, pursuant to which a husband declared that if he did not return within a specified period of time, then his wife was divorced. This divorce was retroactively effected to the time when it was given.[13]

There is a further refinement of these rules. Thus, despite the retroactive effect of the get upon the occurrence of the specified condition, if there was cohabitation between the parties during the period of time from the giving of the get to the occurrence of the specified condition, the get loses its validity. The basis for this rule is the already mentioned presumption "that a man does not cohabit with a woman for the sake of promiscuity." Therefore, we presume that there was thereby an intent by the parties, through such cohabitation, to enter into a *new* marital relationship. The get previously given, therefore, is thereby rendered a "get yashan" (old get), and is invalid.[14]

5. *Attestation.* A get, having been written at the specific request of the husband, must be signed by two competent witnesses.[15]

6. *Delivery.* It is fundamental to Jewish law that a get be physically delivered by the husband, or by his agent, to his wife or her agent, or that it be delivered to a place that is under her actual and physical control.[16] This rule was, of course, effected to assure that the wife has actual or pre-sumptive notice of its contents.[17] Hence, at the time of delivery, the husband or his agent is obligated to inform the wife that a get is being delivered.[18]

7. *Agency.* Under Jewish law, either a husband or a wife may appoint an agent to "give" or "accept" a get.[19] This agency can be revoked, as we discussed above.

Chapter VII
THE GET PROCEDURE
("SEDER HAGET")

The formalities attendant upon the actual writing and delivery of a get are detailed and complex. It is for this reason that the Talmud declared:[1]

> Rabbi Yehudah said in the name of Shmuel, all (Rabbis) who are not intricately versed in the details of marriage and divorce should not participate in divorce proceedings.

We will herein describe the procedure that is generally followed for the writing and delivery of a get and the rules relating thereto, as set forth in *Shulḥan Aruch, Even Ha'ezer,* chapter 154:[2]

(Note.—During the days of the Talmudic Sages, it was the custom to have a man learned in the law preside over the divorce proceeding, and the early Rabbis were accustomed to have the divorce procedure conducted only before the ablest authorities. It is therefore improper for any person to officiate in these matters unless he is learned in the law of marriage and divorce. And if one who is unqualified should endeavor to conduct divorce proceedings, I am of the opinion that his acts should be declared null and void.)[3]

1. It is the custom in some places not to conduct divorce proceedings on Friday.

2. A scribe and two witnesses must be present, neither of whom is related to the other, nor to the husband or the wife. (Note. — . . . The witnesses should be cautioned by the presiding Rabbi to review their lives and repent of any sin that they may have committed, lest through their sinfulness they should be incompetent to act in this proceeding. They should be able to understand the text of the get. If they lack such understanding they should be taught the meaning of the get, its nature, and the requirements thereof, which should be explained to them, to the scribe, as well as to the husband.)

3. The scribe should not be one of the witnesses.

5. It is required that they (the witnesses) should recognize the man and his wife.

7. If the husband is sick, care should be taken to see that he is of sound mind at the time of the writing and delivery of the get.

8. If he desires to couple the divorce with a condition, it should not be mentioned to the scribe or to the subscribing witnesses until the document is delivered.

9. All persons may write the bill of divorce except a deaf-mute, an idiot, a slave, a Gentile, a Jew who has apostatized, or one who willfully and maliciously breaks the Sabbath.

10. The husband himself should not write the get, unless no other person can be obtained to write it.

11. In a like manner the husband should not interfere with the scribe by directing how to write the get.

12. If possible to obtain any other person, no relative of the husband or of the wife should act as scribe.

13. The scribe should furnish the parchment, ink and pen

and all other material, and the husband should perform an act of acquisition (*kinyan*) by lifting them up.

14. The rabbi should ask the husband, "Do you give this get of your own free will, without any compulsion? If you have made any vow or taken any oath which binds you to give this get, tell it to us and we will absolve you from it." The husband should answer, "I have neither vowed nor sworn and I am under no compulsion, but I give this get of my own free will without any compulsion or condition." If the husband should acknowledge that he had in any way bound himself to give the get, he must first be absolved in order that he may act without compulsion. If he has given security that he will divorce his wife, it is not considered tantamount to the above cases, and he is not deemed then to be under restraint or compulsion in the sense above indicated.

15. The husband hands the parchment and the pen and ink to the scribe in the presence of the witnesses, saying to him "Write for me a bill of divorce for my wife . . . . . . the daughter of . . . . . . and for the purpose of separation, and I authorize you to write as many bills as may be necessary until one shall be produced which shall be without flaw both in the writing and in the attestation, in accordance with the opinion of Rabbi. . . . . . ."

16. "And you . . . . . . and . . . . . . be witnesses and attest this get for my wife . . . . . . the daughter of . . . . . . and for the purpose of separation and I authorize you to attest as many bills as may be necessary until one shall be produced which shall be without flaw both in the writing and in the attestation, in accordance with the opinion of Rabbi. . . . . . ."

17. If it be found necessary to write two bills of divorce on account of the doubt as to the proper names of the parties, the scribe and the witnesses shall be specially authorized to do so.

18. The scribe should not write and the witnesses should not sign until they have received the order from the mouth of the husband himself.

19. The husband should pay the fee of the scribe. If he does not, the wife may pay it.

20. The husband should state before the witnesses that he has not raised and will not raise any protest or declaration annulling the get, and that anything which he had said or may say for this purpose shall be null and void, and that any witness who may appear in his behalf shall be declared incompetent to testify.

21. The witnesses in whose presence instructions are given to the scribe should be personally requested to sign the get, and should be present when the names of the parties and the date are written in it.

22. It is necessary that they should know this to be the get which the scribe has written in the name of the husband for the wife, and therefore if they desire to leave after it has been written, they should make a mark on it so that they may be able to identify it.

23. It is advisable that the husband should be present with the scribe and witnesses until it has been written, signed and delivered, that he may not raise any protest against the get or do anything which might tend to invalidate the proceedings.

24. If he desires to send the get to the wife through a messenger, it is necessary that the messenger should be present through the entire proceedings.

25. It is necessary before the get is written that he should be informed that he is to be the messenger and the Rabbi should state in his hearing that this get is written and attested for the woman, in order that the messenger may be afterwards enabled to testify to this fact.

26. When the get is sent by a messenger it is advisable that the husband should be solemnly sworn not to raise any protest against the get or do anything which might invalidate the proceedings and annul the get.

27. The husband and the messenger must be of full age, for a minor can neither act as a messenger nor designate one.

28. The messenger must be neither a deaf-mute, an idiot, a minor, a slave, a Gentile, a blind man, nor one who has been guilty of a transgression of some Biblical commandment.

29. The get should not be delivered by a messenger if the husband and wife are both in the same city.

30. If the husband is obliged to go away and cannot wait until the get is written and signed, let him give his directions as above before a Beth Din, adding the following: "I hereby designate . . . . . . , the son of . . . . . . , a messenger to carry this get to my wife . . . . . . , the daughter of . . . . . . , wherever he may find her, and his hand shall be as my hand and his mouth as my mouth and his act as my act and his delivery as my delivery, and I authorize him to designate any numbers of sub-messengers until the get reaches her hand or the hand of her messenger and as soon as the get reaches her hand or the hand of her messenger from the hand of . . . . . . my messenger or from the hand of any sub-messenger thus designated, she is divorced from me and is permitted to marry any man."

31. He who orders the divorce to be delivered in this manner cannot couple it with conditions.

32. If he desires that the divorce should not go into effect until after a certain period, he must, when ordering the messenger to deliver the get to the wife, state that she will not be divorced thereby until after the fixed period of time has expired.

33. It is not necessary that the messenger should be designated in the presence of the husband, but he may be designated by the witnesses (under the direction of the husband) to act as messenger. (Note—This is true only when the husband, for certain reasons, cannot himself hand the get to the messenger.)

36. Before the scribe begins to write the get, he must ask the husband to give him his name and the name of his father and any surnames that they may have.

37. And it is proper also (where possible) to put the same question to the woman and her father.

38. The scribe and the witnesses must be together during the entire proceeding.

39. The parchment must be cut to the required size before the writing is commenced.

40. If the scribe has made a mistake in writing and begins a new get on the same sheet, he must first cut off the portion of the parchment on which he has written.

41. The parchment should be greater in length than in breadth.

42. It should be ruled with thirteen lines, the last line to be divided into two small lines for the signatures of the witnesses, one under the other.

44. The lines should not be ruled with lead, nor on the same side as the writing.

45. Some say the get should not be written with a quill pen.

46. The writing should be clear and not crooked or confused.

47. The letters should be separated and not joined together.

48. Care should be taken not to have the letters of two lines running into each other.

49. The letters should not extend beyond the marginal line.

50. There must be no erasures of ink spots; in case ink drops into a letter, a new get must be written.

51. If a slip of the pen caused an error, it cannot be erased; a new get must be written.

52. There must be no roughness in the letters, and no writing over erasures.

53. The scribe must be careful to write the form of the get according to the regulation.

54. If the get is found to be improperly written and the husband is still present, he must give the order to write a new one.

55. When the scribe is about to write he must say to the witnesses: "Behold, I write this get in the name of . . . . . ., the son of . . . . . ., for the purpose of divorcing his wife . . . . . ., the daughter of . . . . . .," and then he must proceed to write it at once.

56. The ink must be dry before the witnesses sign.

57. And then they sign one under the other.

58. And in the presence of each other.

59. Each of the witnesses must state before signing, "I sign this get in behalf of . . . . . . the son of . . . . . . for the purpose of divorcing with it . . . . . . the daughter of . . . . . ."

60. The signatures must be placed at the right hand of the sheet next to the margin.

61. Within the space of two lines from the last line in the body of the get.

62. Each witness must sign his own name and the name of his father, thus, ... the son of . . . . . ., witness.

63. The signatures must be clear and distinct.

64. The scribe must not be a witness.

65. The signatures must be dried.

66. The Rabbi and the witnesses must read the get together with the signatures of the witnesses, and after they have read it, the Rabbi must ask the scribe, "Is this the get which you have written at the request of the husband, for the purpose of divorcing his wife . . . . . . the daughter of . . . . . ?" and he answers "Yes." He then asks one of the witnesses, "Did you hear the husband give the order to the scribe to write the get?"

67. "Do you recognize this to be the get?"

68. "Did you sign it at the request of the husband?"

69. "Did you sign it in his behalf and for the purpose of divorcing his wife?"

70. "Do you recognize your signature?"

71. "Did you sign it in the presence of the other witness?"

72. "Do you recognize his signature?"

73. And the witness answers "Yes" to all of these questions; and in the same manner the second witness is interrogated.

74. Then the get is given to the husband and he is asked whether he gives it of his own free will, as above.

75. The husband then repeats the statement made in paragraph 20.

76. If the husband leaves before the delivery of the get, he is sworn not to attempt to invalidate the proceedings, or raise any protest against the get.

78. The Rabbi addresses them, saying: "If any man pres-

ent knows anything to invalidate the get or why it should not be delivered, let him speak before it is delivered; for after it is delivered, I shall pronounce the ban of excommunication upon any one who shall attempt to invalidate the get."

79. The Rabbi calls upon all competent persons to be witnesses.

80. It is advisable that the attesting witnesses should be present at the delivery.

81. The Rabbi shall direct the woman to remove any rings that she may have on her fingers[4] and to stretch forth her hands, open them, bring them together (in front of her) so as to be able to receive the get, and her hands should not be inclined, lest the get fall from them.

(Note— The Rabbi asks her whether she receives the get of her own free will, and she answers "yes." The Rabbi then inquires about the ketubah, and she should return the ketubah [the written document] to her husband, or she should waive the same, to avoid later disputes regarding the ketubah.)

82. Care must be taken that no one assists her in taking the get, and that neither any portion of her clothing, nor any other thing touches her hand as she receives the get.

83. She must not close her hand on it until the husband pronounces the words mentioned in paragraph 84.

84. The husband drops the get into her hands, saying: "This is your get, and you are divorced by it from me, and are permitted to marry any man."

85. After he has placed (dropped) the get in her hands, and has removed his hand therefrom, she closes her hands and lifts them upwards,[5] and then the Rabbi takes it from her and reads it for the second time before the witnesses, and pronounces the ban of excommunication on any one who shall attempt to invalidate it.

86. And then the Rabbi tears the get crosswise.

(Note— And our custom is that the officiating Rabbi retains the get in his possession and does not give it to the divorcee, and this procedure must be followed.)

87. He warns the woman not to become betrothed within ninety days from that date.[6]

88. According to some opinions, the get should be delivered by day and not by night;

89. except in a case of emergency, in which the get may be written and delivered at night. It must be delivered on the same day on which it was written, except when delivery on the same day is impossible.

90. The husband should not remain alone with his wife between the writing and delivery of the get, and if he does so, it becomes an "old get," with which she cannot be divorced.

91. If the get is brought to her by a messenger, it must be delivered to her in the presence of two witnesses, and if the messenger is related to her or otherwise incompetent, it is delivered in the presence of at least three, with this statement: "This is your get which your husband sends you, and by it you are divorced from him and free to marry any man, and this get was written and signed in my presence."

97. If the get is to be delivered to a messenger to carry it to the wife, he is appointed in the presence of two witnesses and it is read to him in their presence, and the scribe and the witnesses make their statements before him, as above (paragraphs 66-80).

98. After this the Rabbi hands the get to the husband and he hands it to the messenger, saying, "Take this get to my wife, wherever you may find her, and your hand shall be as my hand, and your mouth as my mouth, and your act as my act, and your delivery as my delivery, and I authorize you to designate other messengers and sub-messengers until the get

reaches her hand or the hand of her messenger from your hand, or from the hand of your messenger, or from the hand of the messengers of your messengers, etc.," as above (paragraph 30).

99. If the divorce is coupled with conditions, the husband says to the wife at the time of the delivery: "This is your get and you are hereby divorced from me and free to marry any man on condition that if I do not return on this day after twelve months you are divorced from this moment, and if I return within the said period, and appear before . . . and . . . this shall not be a get, and I hereby declare that my wife shall be competent to testify that I have not returned and have not been reunited with her.

100. If the husband is sick he says to her at the time of the delivery, "This is your get and you are divorced by it from me and are free to be married to any man on condition that if I do not die before (a certain day) this shall not be a get, but if I die before that time this shall be a get from this moment."

(Note— . . . and he may thereafter not secrete himself with her unless there is another person present.)[7]

101. One should be very careful not to engage in divorce proceedings unless he is learned in the law of divorce, for there are many points to be considered, and it is easy for a man to err therein, and this would result in invalidating the proceedings and in bastardizing children, and may the Rock of Israel save us from all error, Amen.

Chapter VIII
THE LEGAL CONSEQUENCES
OF DIVORCE

Upon the termination of a marriage, the man and the woman, are free to remarry, as he or she chooses. There are, however, certain limitations.

The divorced woman is not permitted to marry a kohen,[1] nor is she permitted to marry a man with whom she is suspected of having committed adultery.[2] She is also unable to marry any persons who served as witnesses at the delivery of her get,[3] nor, in certain circumstances, may she marry an agent who delivered the get to her on behalf of her husband.[4] A divorcee may not remarry within a period of ninety days after having been divorced; this is so as not to cast any doubt upon the paternity of her first child from the second marriage.[5]

The divorced parties are, again with certain limitations, permitted to remarry each other. Such remarriage is in fact considered a meritorious deed and is permissible for them even during those times when marriages are otherwise prohibited. Thus, although marriages during the intermediate days of the festivals of Passover and Sukkot are not permitted,[6] the remarriage of a divorced couple is permitted.[7]

Remarriage of a divorced couple to each other is prohibited, however, when a man is a kohen, because a kohen may not marry a divorcee. Nor is remarriage permitted where adultery was the grounds for divorce. Also, a divorced couple may not remarry each other if the woman has, in the interim, married somebody else (the second marriage having ended either by death of the husband or by divorce).[8]

A divorce effectuates the ketubah obligations assumed by the husband, discussed above.[9] The wife is entitled to payment of her ketubah, except in those instances where such is forfeited, as well as the return of her own property, as also discussed above.[10]

A divorce also terminates the husband's obligation to provide support and maintenance for his wife and his right of inheritance.[11]

The divorced parties are not permitted to continue to reside in their former common dwelling and, indeed, they must not even seclude themselves in circumstances that might give rise to the implication or perception that they have engaged in sexual relations. This for the reason that there is a presumption that any further sexual relations between them is for the sake of a renewed marriage, rather than for illicit purposes. Therefore, any cohabitation between the parties after divorce will give rise to the presumption that a new marital relationship was intended to be effected by the cohabitation, and a second get will be required. This rule applies even if there is no direct evidence that the parties engaged in sexual relations, and there exists merely the suspicion that they engaged in such relationship.[12]

An unfortunate consequence of divorce, both in secular society as well as in the Jewish community, is the troublesome issue of custody and support obligations for children, after divorce. Briefly stated, under Jewish law, divorce does not relieve a husband from his obligations for the support of the children of his marriage.[13] The mother has the preference to custody of male children up to the age of six, with the father being obligated to provide support.[14] Thereafter, if the mother insists upon continued custody, and the court does not find that such continued custody is essential to the child's best interest, the father may be relieved of further support obligations.[15] As for daughters, the mother has the continued preference of custody, and the father remains obligated for support, even after the mother remarries.[16]

All of these rules, however, are subject to judicial supervision and discretion, depending upon what appears to the judge to be in the best interests of the child,[17] not unlike the approach taken in American courts.[18]

Part II
THE SEARCH
FOR EQUALITY

Chapter IX
THE SEARCH FOR EQUALITY

The attitude of Jewish law regarding the rights of a wife in divorce litigation has been evolving, to a greater or lesser extent, during various periods, since the close of the Talmudic era.[1] From 500 C.E. to 1200 C.E. there were three major attempts to achieve a measure of equality for a wife regarding the giving of a get.

The first of these attempts was a takanah, enacted in the year 650 C.E. This takanah prevailed for a period of approximately 400 years, from 650 C.E. to 1050 C.E., in certain countries, notably Babylonia (Persia) and North Africa. Enacted by the Geonim (Rabbis who flourished up to the 11th century C.E.), the takanah permitted a wife to demand a get in a variety of circumstances, including dislike of or distaste for her husband. The Jewish courts in these communities enjoyed considerable autonomy, and they accordingly utilized the concepts discussed above[2] regarding the right of the Rabbis to annul a marriage in order to compel or to coerce a husband to give a get.

As we previously mentioned, under Jewish law, all who marry do so in accordance with the will of the Rabbis. Therefore, the Rabbis were considered to be vested with authority to indeed annul a marriage where appropriate. The Geonim utilized or invoked this power on the basis of the Talmudic discussion dealing with a rebellious wife, or "moredet," discussed above.[3]

The Mishna[4] sets forth the rules relating to a "moredet" who refuses to engage in sexual relations with her husband, as follows:

> One who rebels against her husband has her ketubah diminished 7 dinarim per week; Rabbi Yehuda says 7 tarpeiken. To what degree is that ketubah diminished? To the full value of her ketubah. Rabbi Yosi says there is a constant diminishing forever, so that even if she were to inherit property from another source, her husband has a claim against it . . .

The Talmud[5] states that a change was made in the above-stated Mishnaic rule to the effect that an announcement was to be made, in the synagogue, on four consecutive Sabbaths, that the wife would thereafter immediately lose her entire ketubah if she did not cease her rebellion (instead of a gradual diminishment thereof, as stated in the Mishna). It also states[6] that she would not be granted a get until a year had passed, in the hope that she would, in the meantime, cease her rebellion.

There is a dispute among the Rabbis of the Talmud as to the motive for a wife's refusal to engage in sexual relations.[7] The text states:

> What type of woman is in the category of "moredet"? Amemar says, it is the woman who says, "I want to remain married, but I am rebelling merely to spite my husband." However, if she says "he is repulsive to me," we do not force her. Mar Zutrah says we force her.

On the basis of this Mishna and the aforesaid discussion of the Rabbis, the following ruling was enacted by Sherira Gaon:[8]

> You have asked with respect to a woman who is living with her husband, but who states to him "I do not wish to live with you." Is the husband obligated to give her aught of her ketubah; is this within the category of "moredet"?
>
> The Gaon answers:
>
> We know that according to the established rule, a man is not forced to divorce his wife at the request of the latter except in those instances in which our Rabbis decided that it was permissible so to do. Thereafter they enacted a takanah that it would be proclaimed for four consecutive weeks and she was warned through Beth Din that she would lose her entire ketubah, and it was then enacted that where she seeks a divorce that she be required to wait twelve months, perhaps she will relent, and if she does not so relent after twelve months, the husband is forced to give a get.
>
> The Gaon continues:
>
> But when the Rabbanan Savorai (predecessors of the Geonim—successors of the Amoraim 503 C.E.—689 C.E. [?]) saw that Jewish women go and attach themselves to the Gentiles, in an attempt to force their husbands to give a get, and sometimes the latter gave gittin under duress and grave questions arose as to whether they are properly being forced to give a get or improperly, and dreadful consequences ensue, it was enacted by (earlier Geonim) . . . that the husband is forced to give a get where the wife seeks a get . . . and we follow this takanah more than 300 years later, and you do the same.

This ruling manifested a well-established Geonic takanah, prevalent in those countries subject to their jurisdiction, pursuant to which an almost total equality was created between a husband and a wife regarding get. Thus, while not abrogating the established rule, that it was only a husband that could give a get, a wife could now petition the court to compel her husband to give her a get.

We see that, during this period of time, Jewish law held that either a husband or a wife could cause the termination of their marriage by obtaining a divorce against the will of the other.[9] The only difference between the man's and the woman's capability of doing this was that the husband could effect the same without recourse to a Beth Din, whereas it was necessary for the wife to seek the aid of the Beth Din for this relief.

Lest it be contended that such takanah was but a temporary deviation, we must point out that its pervasive nature is reflected in certain Genizah texts[10] as continuing in Islamic lands well into the Middle Ages.[11] Unfortunately, however, this Geonic takanah was ultimately rejected by various authorities, on varying grounds. In the 12th Century, the view of Maimonides[12] was that the Geonic takanah had no continuing validity by virtue of its lack of widespread acceptance.[13] Others, notably Naḥmanides[14] and Rabbenu Asher,[15] whilst not questioning the authority of the Geonim to enact this takanah, questioned, however, its advisability, and, in the case of Rabbenu Asher, assumed that it was an emergency measure enacted by them for their own time, and not for future generations.

At the other extreme was the view of Rabbenu Tam,[16] who believed that the Geonim lacked the authority to enact such takanah.[17]

It should be noted, however, that although Maimonides disagreed with the Geonic takanah, he nevertheless formulated a most liberal view in this area, on the basis of the very same Talmudic discussion regarding "moredet," which differs from the Geonic takanah only in its breadth.

In order to better understand Maimonides' view, we shall return to the discussion between the two Amoraim, Amemar and Mar Zutra, regarding the different types of "moredet."[18] Amemar held that the "moredet" whose ketubah is gradually diminished is one who insists that she wants to remain married, and her refusal to engage in sexual relations with her husband is due to mere spite. However, if she claims that he is repulsive to her ("ma'us alay"), then "we do not force her." Mar Zutra opines, however, that "we force her," that is, that we do apply compulsion, by diminishing her ketubah as a means of curbing her rebellion, even where she asserts that her husband is repulsive to her.

The interpretation of this controversy has engendered much discussion. Thus, Rashi[19] and others, including Maimonides, interpret Amemar's view as holding that in cases of spitework we apply compulsion to the wife to desist in her behavior by diminishing her ketubah. However, in the case of "ma'us alay" (he is repulsive to me), "we do not force her to remain with him, but he gives her a get and she leaves without a ketubah."[20]

Maimonides put the matter thusly:[21]

> A woman who refuses to have sexual relations with her husband is a *moredet*. (In such circumstances) we ask her why she is rebelling? If she says it is because "He is repulsive to me (*ma'astihu*) and I am unwilling voluntarily to engage in conjugal relationships with him," we force him to divorce her immediately, for she is not as a slave that she should be forced to have intercourse with one who is hateful to her. And she leaves without a ketubah . . .

This second approach similarly went far towards equalizing the position of men and women. We previously saw that, under the view of the Geonim, there was almost total equality between the sexes regarding the giving of a get. Under the view of Maimonides there was similarly almost complete equality between the sexes with regard to a get where sexual relations with her husband was repulsive to the wife, or where the wife manifested intense dislike or hatred of her husband.[22]

However, the view of Maimonides in this matter has been almost universally rejected. Rabbenu Asher[23] points out that Rabbenu Tam and others disagreed with Maimonides and he adds:

> . . . and the views of Maimonides are even more perplexing . . . how can one justify forcing a husband to give a get and to set a married woman free (merely because she is not willing to have sexual relationships with her husband)? Let her not have relationships with him and let her remain an eternal widow, for she is not commanded to beget children and merely because she desires to follow the fancy of her heart and has cast her eyes upon another and desires him more than the husband of her youth shall we give in to her lusts and force her husband who loves the wife of his youth to divorce her? G-d forbid!

Thus, some authorities, including Rabbenu Tam,[24] maintain that a husband is never forced to give a get on the ground of "ma'us alay." Other authorities follow the view of Maimonides and require a husband to give a get where the wife is able to give adequate substantiation (*amatla*) for her request for a get on that ground.[25]

It is therefore quite unfortunate that, as with the Geonic takanah, the view of Maimonides was similarly and almost universally rejected.[26]

We have discussed two early attempts, both ultimately unsuccessful, to equalize the status of husband and wife as regards get. The third and final attempt, although more limited in scope, proved the most successful to date.

In the 11th Century, a takanah was enacted that was generally attributed to Rabbenu Gershom, and was popularly known as the "Herem of Rabbenu Gershom." Under this takanah, a husband was prohibited from divorcing his wife against her will, except in certain limited circumstances, which will be discussed below.[27]

It is indeed worthy of note that Rabbenu Gershom himself accepted the validity of the takanah of the Geonim, who were his contemporaries.[28]

The application of the Geonic takanah (if it had not been rejected later) in conjunction with the takanah of Rabbenu Gershom, would, indeed, have resulted in a most favored position for Jewish women, for they could then demand a get against the will of their husbands, but they could not have been divorced without their own consent.[29]

Nevertheless, and even aside from the continued validity of the Geonic takanah, the Herem of Rabbenu Gershom alone greatly enhanced the position of women. As pointed out by Rabbenu Asher in this regard:[30]

> When he (Rabbenu Gershom) saw how the generation was abusive of Jewish daughters insofar as divorcing them under compulsion *he enacted that the rights of women be equal to those of men*, and just as a man divorces only from his own will, so too, a woman might henceforth be divorced only willingly . . . (emphasis supplied).

There was another takanah enacted at about the same

Divorce In Jewish Law and Life

time, similarly attributed to Rabbenu Gershom, and also regarding marriage. This was a takanah which prohibited polygamy.[31]

These two takanot of Rabbenu Gershom, taken together, prevented a husband from divorcing his wife against her will, and consequently from marrying another during the continued subsistence of the marriage. Jewish law, however, limited the polygamy takanah by allowing a husband to take a second wife where, for instance, his first wife was incompetent, and hence unable to accept a get, if he first obtained the permission of one hundred Rabbis.[32] Similarly, if a wife refused to accept a get (after the takanah of Rabbenu Gershom), but the husband had the right to divorce her, as in the case of a "moredet," it was held that Rabbenu Gershom's takanah was not applicable and the husband was permitted to divorce her against her will.[33]

If a husband improperly violated the takanah of Rabbenu Gershom, and divorced his wife by giving her a get against her will, it was established that he remains obligated to support his wife, and he may not remarry. The wife, if she so chooses, may either continue to look to her "husband" for support, or she may remarry, in which case, of course, her former husband's obligations to her cease, and he may then also remarry.[34]

Thus, up until modern times, it was the takanah or Herem of Rabbenu Gershom which provided a wife with her basic protection with regard to a get. We turn now to modern-day problems affecting the rules relating to get, and the responses of Jewish law towards such problems.

Part III
JEWISH DIVORCE IN THE 19TH AND 20TH CENTURIES

PROBLEMS
AND RESPONSES

Chapter X
CIVIL VS. RELIGIOUS DIVORCE

Civil divorce did not exist until comparatively recently. For the most part, during the first half of the Middle Ages in Europe, divorce, under the influence of Christianity, was almost non-existent, and was subject to the jurisdiction of the ecclesiastical courts. Insofar as the Jews were concerned, the European states in which they resided permitted them to exercise jurisdiction over themselves in the areas of marriage and divorce. There was thus no occasion for any conflict between Jewish law of divorce and secular law.

In the 16th Century a new development arose which created new problems for Jewish divorce, whose reverberations are still being felt today.

Secular divorce was first recognized in Scotland in 1573,[1] and in France in 1792.[2] It was later recognized in European nations and elsewhere.[3] This raised the spectre, horrid indeed from the point of view of Jewish law, that a Jewish couple could be deemed to be divorced by the laws of the state or country in which they lived, and yet remain married in the eyes of Jewish law, unless a get was given and accepted.

The developments in this area in France are particularly

relevant to an understanding of the problems inherent in the conflict between Jewish and secular divorce, and the response of Jewish law to that conflict.

As noted above, France was second only to Scotland as a Catholic country that broke with Canonical law and allowed secular divorce upon certain specific grounds. After the French Revolution, French law underwent a modification, the result being abolition of secular divorce in 1816.[4] However, secular divorce was renewed in France in 1852, and remains in force today.[5] The first attempt by the French Rabbis to solve the problems inherent in the clash between religious and secular divorce was most simplistic. In 1885 it was suggested that, upon the civil termination of a marriage by secular divorce, the marriage be considered dissolved under Jewish law as well.[6] This suggestion was rejected on the ground that the termination of a marriage validly entered into under Jewish law could be effectuated in no other manner than by the giving of a get.[7]

Several further attempts to reconcile the demands of Jewish law with secular divorce were made by the French Rabbis; all of them with similar rejection.

In 1893 it was suggested that marriage be henceforth conditioned on the religious termination of the marriage by get in the event of a secular divorce. If, in fact, the husband or wife, upon the civil termination of their marriage by secular divorce, refused to give or accept a get respectively, the marriage was then annulled retroactively. This proposal was likewise rejected,[8] but was revived, in a slightly modified framework, and again presented by the French Rabbis in 1907. This too was rejected, because it was considered inappropriate to attach such a condition to a marriage.[9]

There were a number of further, sporadic attempts to

reapply the concept of conditional marriage, none of which met with any favor.[10]

One further suggestion, although similarly rejected, is worthy of note. After having perceived that the concept of a conditional marriage proved to be ineffectual in the attempt to provide a resolution of the clash between civil and religious divorce, Rabbi Louis Epstein suggested that the concept of Agency, well known in Jewish law generally as well as in divorce law,[11] be utilized.[12] He suggested that, immediately subsequent to the marriage ceremony, the husband appoint his wife as an agent to have a get written and delivered to herself, on her husband's behalf. Thus, in the event of a civil divorce, the wife could exercise the agency authority previously conferred upon her by her husband, and she could have the get written and delivered to herself as her husband's agent.

This approach too was quite resoundingly rejected by Rabbinic authorities on various grounds, including the not-insubstantial basis that cohabitation of the parties during the marriage totally invalidated the agency.[13]

The next substantial development in this area of Jewish law came in 1954. It is to this that we shall now turn.

Chapter XI
THE CONSERVATIVE KETUBAH

The alarming rise in the divorce rate in recent years has exacerbated the problems created by the interplay and clash between secular and religious divorce. Because it is absolutely essential under Jewish law that a marriage validly entered into be terminated by a get, the unfortunate result has been that there are numerous instances in which one spouse, usually, but not invariably, the wife, has been unable to remarry after the civil termination of the marriage by virtue of the refusal of the other spouse to give or to accept a get.

Modern attempts to resolve this problem have been varied. All, however, have met with but minimal degrees of success, if any.

The first major attempt to resolve this problem in recent years was the Conservative Ketubah. We have previously, in chapter II, above, discussed the traditional ketubah. The modifications to the traditional ketubah introduced by the Conservative movement in 1954 have a two-fold importance for our own study.

Firstly, the Conservative Ketubah, despite its deficiencies, represents a major contribution towards an attempted resolution of the problems inherent in the application of Jewish law in a secular society. Moreover, and of more crucial consequence, the type of agreement represented by the Conservative Ketubah may contain the basis for a projected viable solution of this problem, one which would be acceptable to *all* branches of Judaism, both in the the United States and elsewhere.

In 1954, the Conference on Jewish Law, a joint body created by the Jewish Theological Seminary of America and the Rabbinical Assembly of America (organs of the Conservative branch of American Judaism), formulated the following addition to, or modification of, the traditional ketubah:[1]

> And in solemn assent to their mutual responsibilities and love, the bridegroom and bride have declared: as evidence of our desire to enable each other to live in accordance with the Jewish Law of Marriage throughout our lifetime, we, the bride and bridegroom, attach our signatures to this Ketubah, and hereby agree to recognize the Beth Din of the Rabbinical Assembly and the Jewish Theological Seminary of America, or its duly appointed representatives, as having authority to counsel us in the light of Jewish tradition which requires husband and wife to give each other complete love and devotion, and to summon either party at the request of the other, in order to enable the party so requesting to live in accordance with the standards of the Jewish Law of Marriage throughout his or her lifetime. We authorize the Beth Din to impose such terms of compensation as it may see fit for failure to respond to its summons or to carry out its decision.

It was the apparent intention of the authors of this agreement to provide a vehicle for the amelioration of the problem under consideration. Thus, contemplating the possibility that the parties to a marriage might someday be civilly divorced, they had the parties enter into what was, in effect, an arbitration agreement, pursuant to which they agreed to submit to the Beth Din of the Rabbinical Assembly and Jewish Theological Seminary for counselling:

> in order to enable the party so requesting to live in accordance with the standards of the Jewish Law of Marriage throughout his or her lifetime.

Although not specifically so stated, it was the obvious purpose of this agreement to assure that the parties obtain a get after the civil termination of their marriage, thereby permitting the husband and wife to remarry under Jewish law and to continue to live in accordance with its standards. Therefore, in the event that one spouse refused to participate in a get proceeding, he or she could be summoned by the other spouse to what was, in effect, an arbitration proceeding, at which the recalcitrant spouse would be requested or directed to permit the other spouse to live in accordance with the standards of Jewish law, by either giving or accepting a get.

It was also intended that, absent voluntary compliance by the reluctant spouse with the request or direction of the Beth Din, court enforcement of the Beth Din's decision would be sought and, hopefully, obtained.

This agreement was immediately criticized on various grounds.

Questions were raised regarding its enforceability in the secular courts,[2] as well as its validity under Jewish law.[3] The first-mentioned question, however, may have been resolved by the recent decision of the New York Court of Appeals in the case of *AVITZUR v. AVITZUR*, to be discussed in the next chapter.

Chapter XII
THE GET IN AMERICAN COURTS

In recent years, individuals embroiled in divorce litigation have turned with increasing frequency to the civil courts to seek to compel a recalcitrant spouse to either give or accept a get. The courts have, over the years, exhibited a varying degree of inclination towards compelling the giving or acceptance of a get, depending upon the circumstances. The reported cases have involved the following situations:

1. Where an agreement existed, either oral or written, and either pre-nuptial or post-nuptial, for the procurement of a get after the granting of a civil divorce.

2. Where an agreement existed, either pre-nuptial or post-nuptial, to submit the issue of procurement of a get to Rabbinical arbitration.

3. Where no formal agreement of the types referred to in items 1-2 existed, but aid of the secular courts is invoked on the basis of the provisions in the traditional ketubah.

4. Where the aid of the secular court is invoked to aid the procurement of a get pursuant to a decree of a court of the State of Israel.

1. Agreements, either oral or written, and either pre-nuptial or post-nuptial, for the procurement of a get after civil divorce.

The first reported case involving an agreement to give a get was *PRICE v. PRICE*.[1] In that case, the wife sued upon an agreement prior to marriage which provided that, in the event of a civil divorce, the husband would give her a get. The husband reneged on the agreement and the wife sued for specific performance, asking that the court direct the husband to give the get, as agreed. The court denied the request and held:

> We cannot direct [the husband] to submit himself to a Rabbi for the purpose of procuring a divorce and we certainly cannot direct (as is prayed) that he must consent to be divorced. The civil tribunals are certainly without authority to order one to follow the practices of his faith. This is a matter dependent entirely upon his conscience, or upon his religious belief.

In a later New York case, the wife obtained, temporarily at least, the support of the court in a similar circumstance. Thus, in the case of *KOEPPEL v. KOEPPEL*,[2] the parties in a pre-annulment agreement had agreed that the husband, upon the civil dissolution of the marriage, would do the necessary to give his wife a get. The wife sued to compel the husband to comply with the agreement. The court upheld the agreement as against constitutional objection and stated:[3]

> In his opposing affidavit and brief, defendant has raised several general objections to the entire action which will now be discussed. Defendant claims that the entire action is academic in that plaintiff has already remarried and, in fact, is now on her honeymoon. It is not disclosed, however, whether plaintiff was remarried at a civil ceremony or at a religious ceremony in accordance with the rules of

her faith. This action may not be academic to the plaintiff. Nor can it be said that a religious ceremony is of very little importance to the plaintiff if she was willing to marry at a civil ceremony. It may well be that plaintiff has not lived up to the laws of her faith, but this should not forever bar her from rectifying the situation, if she so desires.

Defendant has also contended that a decree of specific performance would interfere with his freedom of religion under the Constitution. Complying with his agreement would not compel the defendant to practice any religion, not even the Jewish faith to which he still admits adherence (paragraph Second of the complaint not denied in the answer). His appearance before the Rabbinate to answer questions and give evidence needed by them to make a decision is not a profession of faith. Specific performance herein would merely require the defendant to do what he voluntarily agreed to do.

Defendant's statement that the ceremony before the Rabbinate takes from two to two and one-half hours is not worthy of discussion. That is not much out of a lifetime, especially if it will bring peace of mind and conscience to one whom defendant must at one time have loved.

Unfortunately, however, after a trial of the action, the agreement was ultimately held to be too indefinite and, hence, unenforceable by the court.[4] It should be noted, however, that the unwillingness of the court to uphold the agreement in this case was, at least in part, predicated upon the fact, quoted above, that the wife had remarried without her get. The Appelate Court noted that the right of the wife to require the husband to participate in the divorce under the agreement was not "absolute," but was to be exercised only when "necessary." The court, apparently on the basis of the wife's remarriage, concluded that such "necessity" under the agreement was not established.

In a more recent case, however, the courts have upheld the validity of an agreement to give a get. Thus, in *WAXSTEIN v. WAXSTEIN*,[5] the lower court, by Justice Heller, granted specific performance of an agreement by a husband to give a get where such agreement was incorporated into a written separation agreement. The decision was affirmed on appeal in a quite cryptic memorandum:[6]

> Under the peculiar circumstances revealed by this record, the determination of (the lower court) was correct.

Although not explicitly so stated by the Appellate Court, the "peculiar circumstances" may have consisted, in part, of the fact that the wife already complied with certain other portions of the agreement. Thus, the agreement, in addition to providing for the giving of a get by the husband, also provided that the wife vacate the marital abode, and transfer title to the house and to certain stock to the husband. The lower court, and apparently the Appellate Court as well, found it unfair for the husband to take advantage of certain portions of the agreement relating to the house and stock, without complying with the portion relating to the get as well.[7]

In one case, the tables were turned, and it was the wife who refused to accept the get. The parties had executed a separation agreement which made support and alimony contingent upon the wife's acceptance of a get. The wife sued for support under the agreement. The court, in *RUBIN v. RUBIN*,[8] in a scholarly decision by Judge Gartenstein, upheld the validity of the agreement, but refused to enforce the support provisions until the get was accepted.

In that decision, Judge Gartenstein discussed the Jewish law of divorce and noted the fact, referred to above,[9] that a get, unlike secular divorce, is not a judicial act, but is, rather, a personal civil act between husband and wife. In discussing the role of the Beth Din and the parties with respect to get procedure, the judge noted:[10]

The foregoing is not to imply that the function of the court was nil or that the get was within the sole province of the husband. Indeed, where grounds existed, the Beth Din (religious court) was convened at the suit of the wife for injunctive relief directing the husband to execute and cause delivery of the get freeing her. On the other hand, even where proceedings were at the instance of the husband, the staggering minutia of technical details requiring the assistance of experts (Kiddushin, 6a, supra), gave the rabbinical courts a *res* upon which to seize in acquiring judicial powers.

Jewish Law is framed on the theory that a dead marriage should be dissolved. While divorce by consent (the Talmud recognized no-fault divorce 2000 years ago) is the outgrowth of this attitude, the rabbinical authorities always took great pains to insure that the marriage was really dead and that the parties were afforded every opportunity to turn back. In this spirit, the procedural minutia involved in the execution and delivery of the get became the vehicle wherein the religious courts assumed their judicial function. For, with the power to lend or withhold that expertise of those "learned in the law" as required by Kiddushin, 6a, the execution and delivery of a get became virtually impossible without the help of the rabbinical court which was extended or withheld depending on the existence of specified grounds when mutual consent was not manifested. In the process of exercising this "judicial" function, rabbinical courts developed the principle that no wife was to be divorced against her will unless certain grounds existed. This practice of rabbinical law, in existence for about a thousand years from earliest Talmudic times, was codified by Rabbenu Gershom in the approximate year 1000 of the common calendar.

Obviously, the get has the same importance today as it has had over the centuries because, in the absence thereof, any remarriage takes place without capacity to contract. Since the party entering the new liaison is already married under ecclesiastical law, cohabitation with the new spouse is adulterous. Finally, to complete this caveat, even if the first marriage is then dissolved by valid get, Jewish religious law prohibits marriage to a person with whom adultery has been committed. This can result in a religious prohibition against marrying the very same second spouse with whom a party has in fact been living.

With respect to constitutional objections, the court reasoned as follows:[11]

> . . . this court is not called upon to enforce this religious discipline against a recalcitrant party, but, rather, is being called upon by the *defaulting* party to enforce the other relief in her favor at a time when she refuses to perform a condition precedent thereto, which happens to be an act of religious significance. The condition precedent could well have been anything else made crucial by agreement of the parties. In this latter instance, where one party to an agreement calling for a get declines to perform, the court will either refuse any relief to the defaulting party, or will hold any application for the same in abeyance pending performance of the obligations assumed pertaining to the get.

It is thus quite apparent from the *WAXSTEIN* and *RUBIN* decisions that the courts will not hesitate to force a party to adhere to an agreement to give a get where that same party wishes to benefit from other portions of that same agreement, as with respect to alimony, or support rights, rights to property, and the like.

A similar situation was presented in *B. v B.*[12] In that case, a husband agreed to give a get in the course of a settlement agreement entered into in civil divorce proceedings and he thereafter reneged on such agreement. Justice Blyn, in his decision, indicated that he might set aside the civil divorce on the ground of fraud and set a hearing for such purposes. In so holding, the court noted that the agreement to give a get constituted one of the vital terms of the agreement and that a serious question therefore existed as to whether the judgment of divorce was induced by fraud on the part of the husband.[13]

This, then, is another instance of the refusal by the court to permit a party to obtain the benefits of part of an agreement (for example, right to civil divorce) without permitting the other party to obtain the reciprocally sought-for other benefits of that same agreement (for example, right to a get).

Thus far we have dealt with agreements, either pre- or post-nuptial, to give a get, that have been reduced to writing. In one case there was an oral stipulation, entered into in open court, pursuant to which a husband agreed to give his wife a get. In *MARGULIES V. MARGULIES,*[14] the husband stipulated orally, in open court, to give a get. The stipulation also encompassed visitation rights and disposition of property. The husband then refused to comply with the portion of the agreement relating to the get, and he was held in contempt and fined by the lower court for his refusal to abide by his agreement. On appeal, the court would not jail the husband for contempt of court for failure to honor the agreement, but did permit the fine to stand on procedural grounds. In so holding, the court pointed out that the husband had benefited from certain portions of the agreement in that he had remarried. It would therefore not permit him to refuse to comply with other portions of that same agreement. Although the court would not permit the husband to be jailed, in upholding the fines for contempt the court stated:[15]

> In any event, there was abundant basis upon which to conclude that defendant's behavior was contumacious. Immediately after the open court stipulation was entered into, defendant, who has remarried, and who accepted the benefits of the agreement, disavowed his representations made in open court. At the time when he agreed to participate in the religious divorce he was well aware of the consequences and nature of the act and that it could only be obtained upon his assertion to the rabbinical court that it was being sought of his own free will. Defendant was also well aware that plaintiff could not enter into a valid remarriage under Jewish law until the "get" had been granted. It is not indicated that any subsequent developments caused defendant to change his mind and upon this record we can only conclude that defendant never intended to carry out the terms of the open court stipulation and that he utilized the court for his own ulterior motives. Such behavior may not be countenanced.

The foregoing reflects quite conclusively that the courts in New York are ready to enforce written or oral agreements to give a get in a variety of circumstances.[16] The implication of this development for the public at large, as well as for the legal profession, will be more fully discussed below.[17]

2. Agreements, either pre- or post-nuptial, to submit to Rabbinical arbitration the issue of procurement of a get.

In the first portion of this chapter we dealt with agreements to give a get. We shall deal now with agreements which are two-tiered. The first tier relates to an agreement to submit the issue of procurement of a get to Rabbinical arbitration. Then, assuming a resolution of the issue by the Rabbinical arbitration panel, the next step would be for one side or the other to ask the court to confirm or to reject the decision of the arbitrators; in New York under the applicable provisions of Article 75 of the Civil Practice Law and Rules.

The merits of this approach are many, from the points of view of both Jewish and American law.

In the type of situation presented by the previously discussed agreement to give a get, one of the parties, usually but not invariably the wife, is asking the court to enforce such agreement. This attempt is fraught with constitutional and First Amendment problems, dealt with by the courts. Moreover, as indeed discussed in several cases,[18] and of more crucial consequence, any get so given under compulsion of the secular courts is subject to grave questions regarding its validity. Because (as we have previously pointed out)[19] a get given under compulsion of a Gentile court is invalid, even if the husband would have been otherwise obligated, under Jewish law, to give the get, it follows therefore that even if the husband complied with the order of the secular court and gave the get, its validity would be questionable.

As such, it clearly appears that the preferred and optimum approach would be to seek to have court enforcement of a decision of a Rabbinical arbitration tribunal directing the giving of a get. For then, and assuming the arbitration panel directs the giving of a get, the function of the secular court would be merely to enforce the decision of the Rabbinical panel, and, as such, would be valid under Jewish law.

Unfortunately, this approach, although most desirable from the point of view of Jewish law, has only recently found favor with the courts of New York State.

In the first case on this point, *PAL v. PAL*,[20] the parties agreed that they would submit themselves to Rabbinical arbitration on the question of whether the husband should give a get. They also agreed that they would each pick a member of the panel and that if they could not agree on the third member of the panel, the court could do so.

The parties were unable to agree on the third member of the panel, and the lower court therefore, pursuant to the agreement, proceeded to choose the third member of the panel. Thereafter, the lower court directed the parties to submit to arbitration pursuant to the agreement.

In these circumstances, of course, and under this type of agreement, the function of the court in the first instance was merely to compel the parties to submit to arbitration, pursuant to a contractual agreement voluntarily entered into. As such, it would, or might, have been anticipated that this would pose no constitutional or First Amendment objections, since the court is not enforcing any religious objectives, but is, instead, enforcing a contractual obligation to submit to arbitration voluntarily entered into. In addition, if, ultimately, the Rabbinical panel concluded that the husband was obligated to give a get, the civil court's function would only be to enforce the decision of the arbitrators-Rabbis. This again should, arguably at least, have no constitutional or First Amendment implications. In addition, and from the point of view of Jewish law, since the enforcement by the civil court of the arbitrator's decision is an application of the concept of a Gentile court requiring a husband to adhere to the valid dictates of a Jewish court, a get so given would be considered valid.

However, the court in *PAL v. PAL* felt otherwise. It refused to enforce the agreement, and stated:[21]

(The lower court) had no authority to, in effect, convene a Rabbinical tribunal (cf. *MARGULIES v. MARGULIES*, 42 A.D. 2d 517, 344 N.Y.S. 2d 482).

In an eloquent, well-reasoned, and scholarly dissent Justice Martuscello argued vigorously, if vainly, for enforcement of the agreement.

The basis for the majority decision, denying enforcement of the agreement, is questionable, particularly in light of the court's own reference to the *MARGULIES* case,[22] which enforced an oral agreement to give a get, as noted above.

The case of *AVITZUR v. AVITZUR*[23] is the first reported case to date involving the Conservative Ketubah. At issue was the question whether the court should direct the parties to proceed to arbitration under the arbitration clause in the ketubah.

In this case, the wife sought an order directing her husband to proceed to arbitration under the terms of the ketubah, to determine whether she was entitled to a get. The husband moved to dismiss the action or, in the alternative, for summary judgment on various grounds, including the ground that:[24]

> ... the lawsuit is so intertwined with religious matters that historically beginning with the First Amendment of the Constitution of the United States and of Article I, Section 3 of the Constitution of the State of New York, both of which guarantee religious freedom, the Courts of this State will take a hands off policy.

The lower court rejected this argument and stated:[25]

> ... This court takes the opposite view, that the relief sought in this suit, if the alleged contract is in fact found to

be an enforceable one, would merely require a decree of this court of specific performance which would relegate the party so ordered to submit himself for a determination of religious law to a religious tribunal as purportedly agreed to by him in the basic premarital papers.

The lower court then denied the husband's motion, as well as the wife's motion for summary judgment, and stated that the issues presented, including the interpretation of the agreement to arbitrate, would be resolved at a full trial.[26]

The husband appealed to the Appellate Division, which reversed the decision of the lower court.[27] The Appellate Court alluded to the facts underlying this case and pointed out that the parties had been married in May, 1966, that they had signed the Conservative Ketubah as part of the marriage ceremony, and that the husband obtained a civil divorce in 1978 on the ground of cruel and inhuman treatment. In rendering its decision, the Appellate Court stated:[28]

> The State having already granted the parties a civil divorce, has no further interest in their marital status. It would thus be a dangerous precedent to allow State Courts to enforce liturgical agreements concerning matters about which the State has no remaining concern.

In so doing, the court distinguished the cases discussed earlier in this chapter, in which the court directed the giving or acceptance of a get, on the ground that such cases:[29]

> ... involved situations where the Ketubah's terms had been incorporated in a subsequent civil agreement.

Mrs. Avitzur took an appeal to the Court of Appeals, New

York's highest court, and that court, in a 4 to 3 decision, reversed the decision of the Appellate Division.[30]

The court held that there was nothing in law or public policy to prevent judicial recognition and, indeed, enforcement of the secular terms of the ketubah. The agreement in the ketubah pursuant to which the parties agreed to submit the issue of the giving of a get to Rabbinical arbitration was viewed by a majority of the Court of Appeals as constituting a secular or neutral agreement properly subject to enforcement by a State court.

In so holding the court stated:

> This agreement—the Ketubah—should ordinarily be entitled to no less dignity than any other civil contract to submit a dispute to a nonjudicial forum, so long as its enforcement violates neither the law nor the public policy of this State.

The Court of Appeals, in disposing of constitutional objections raised by the husband, conceded that the ketubah was a document that had a religious character and that it was entered into as part of a religious wedding ceremony. It nevertheless held that the secular portions thereof were properly enforced under the "neutral principles of law" approach, sanctioned by the Supreme Court of the United States. Such approach, stated the Court of Appeals,

> contemplates the application of objective, well-established principles of secular law to the dispute . . ., thus permitting judicial involvement to the extent that it can be accomplished in purely secular terms.

In applying such approach in this case, the Court of Appeals concluded:

The present case can be decided solely upon the application of neutral principles of contract law, without reference to any religious principle. Consequently, defendant's objections to enforcement of his promise to appear
before the Beth Din, based as they are upon the religious
origin of the agreement, pose no constitutional barrier to
the relief sought by plaintiff. The fact that the agreement
was entered into as part of a religious ceremony does not
render it unenforceable. . . . The courts may properly enforce so much of this agreement as is not in contravention
of law or public policy.

In short, the relief sought by plaintiff in this action is
simply to compel defendant to perform a secular
obligation to which he contractually bound himself.

The dissenting judges, on the other hand, were of the
opinion that the agreement in question was not subject to
enforcement in the civil courts.

Unlike the majority of the court, who viewed the arbitration agreement as being an essentially secular agreement in
a document otherwise religious in character, the minority
looked to the question of the ultimate enforceability by the
civil courts of a decision of the Rabbinical Arbitration Panel
regarding the giving of a get.

In so doing and in applying the reasoning of the decision
of the Appellate Division discussed above, the minority
stated:

. . . the evident objective of the present action —as recognized by the majority and irrefutably demonstrated by the
complaint—even if procedural jurisdiction were to be
assumed, is to obtain a religious divorce, a matter well
beyond the authority of any civil court.

3. *Invocation of the aid of the secular courts on the basis*

*of the provisions of the traditional ketubah where no formal
agreement to give or accept a get exists.*

The oft-tragic consequences of the inability of a wife to
obtain a get after the civil termination of her marriage have
engendered much legal ingenuity on the part of astute counsel in fashioning appropriate remedies.

We have earlier discussed situations involving pre- or
post-marital agreements, either oral or written, to either give
or accept a get, or to submit to arbitration as to whether one
spouse or the other is entitled to the same. However, what of
those situations where no such agreement, in any form,
exists?

It was first argued by astute Canadian counsel that, in
those circumstances, the terms of the traditional ketubah,
discussed and quoted above,[31] afforded a basis for a civil
court to compel a husband to give a get after the civil
dissolution of his marriage. In a leading Canadian case it was
contended by counsel that, as with any other contract, a
ketubah could be enforced by the courts. The lower court, in
fact, accepted this argument and held that the ketubah constituted an implied undertaking by the husband to give a get
where a civil divorce had been granted.[32] Unfortunately,
however, the decision was reversed on appeal.[33]

This argument has, however, found greater favor in the
eyes of judges in the United States.

In a recent and articulate decision by Justice Held, in the
case of *STERN v. STERN*,[34] he agreed with this argument and
directed the husband to give a get. In reaching this conclusion, Justice Held stated that the agreement in the ketubah,
whereby the parties bound themselves to conform to the
"laws of Moses and Israel," obligated the husband in that
case to give his wife a get.

A similar result was reached by a New Jersey court in the case of *MINKIN v. MINKIN.*[35]

In that case, the wife sought to obtain an order directing the husband to obtain and pay for the costs of a get. The court, as in the *STERN* case, assumed that under the terms of the ketubah, and particularly under the portion thereof to the effect that "they agreed to conform to the provisions of the laws of Moses and Israel," the husband was obligated to give his wife a get.

The court also concluded that this did not violate the constitutional and First Amendment rights of the husband.

It must be conceded that the validity of the approach taken by the courts in *STERN* and *MINKIN* is seriously open to question, however commendable the result may be in such cases. In addition, as with the type of situation involving agreements to give a get, there remains the question as to whether a get so given under compulsion of a secular court decree would be valid under Jewish law.

4. *The enforceability of a decree of a court of the State of Israel directing a husband to give a get.*

An interesting and unique situation, but one which is not likely to arise with any frequency, was presented in the case of *SHAPIRO v. SHAPIRO.*[36]

In that case, the parties were married in France in 1959, and moved to Israel, where their two children were born. In 1962, the wife applied to the Israel Rabbinical Courts, which have the sole jurisdiction in matters of marriage and divorce for Jewish residents of Israel, for a get. It was thereafter agreed that the parties would remain separated for six months, and that, at the end of that period, if the wife persisted in her demand for a get, the husband would grant her one. The husband was not to leave the country until the divorce proceedings were terminated. After the six months period, the wife requested her get. However, the husband left the country and, since 1963, did not support either his wife or his children. He became a resident of Brooklyn, New York, and it was there that he was found by his wife.

In the interim (1979), the wife had obtained an order of the Rabbinical Court for the District of Tel Aviv (the Beth Din) directing the husband to give a get.

The wife brought an action in Kings County Supreme Court seeking an order enforcing the order of the Tel Aviv Court, and directing her husband to comply by giving her a get. She was successful in her suit, which was decided in the lower court on traditional legal principles. The lower court, by Justice Hirsh, reasoned that the order of the Tel Aviv Rabbinical Court was an official court order of a foreign state, and that principles of comity (courtesy between states and nations) compelled the conclusion that the Supreme Court in Kings County should enforce the decree of the Rabbinical Court in Tel Aviv. The court concluded:[37]

> Defendant is ordered to schedule an appointment with the Rabbinical Council of America and he is to perform all the ritual acts of the "get" ceremony in accordance with the directions of the Rabbinical Court.

On appeal, the decision of the lower court was affirmed in all respects relevant herein.[38]

This decision is, of course, very refreshing and correct and will provide adequate relief in the isolated instances in which it will again be relevant. It is, of course, most noteworthy that the decision in this case appears to avoid the shoals of all constitutional objections, since it merely enforces a valid order or judgment of a foreign state. In addition, of even more crucial consequence is the fact that a get so given, under the compulsion of the Supreme Court of Kings County, would be valid under Jewish law as well, since the Supreme Court is merely enforcing the order of the Rabbinical Court in Israel.

Having thus reviewed the state of the law in New York and elsewhere, it will be profitable to review the status of the developments in Israel in this area. It is to this subject that we shall now turn.

Chapter XIII
ISRAELI COURTS
AND GET LITIGATION

It is indeed unfortunate that, even in Israel today, where Jewish law governs marriage and divorce for the first time in approximately 1600 years, there are yet many people who are unable to remarry because of their inability to give or obtain a get.[1]

In modern day Israel, matters involving marriage and divorce are within the jurisdiction of the Rabbinic Courts (Battei Din). These courts have the unique power, unavailable elsewhere in the world,[2] to compel the giving or acceptance of a get, when called for by Jewish law, through the use of fines, or imprisonment, or both. And yet, even these means of compulsion have proven to be inadequate.

When it is the wife who refuses to accept a get, a lesser problem is presented, since, if the law mandates that she accept the get, the Beth Din can permit her husband to give it to her against her will. As pointed out above,[3] the takanah of Rabbenu Gershom is inapplicable where the husband is otherwise entitled to divorce his wife as a matter of law, and, hence, the Beth Din can properly, in such circumstances, permit a wife to be divorced against her will.[4] It is a more serious problem, therefore, when it is the wife who seeks the get. Quite often, even the imposition of fines and/or imprisonment are not enough to compel the husband to give a get.

As we also pointed out above,[5] even when compulsion is permitted under Jewish law in order to force a husband to give his wife a get, the husband must nevertheless formally declare his willingness to give a get. If, however, despite the compulsion, the husband still stubbornly refuses to give his consent to the giving of the get, there is nothing that the court can do.[6]

This is exemplified in Israel by instances of stubborn husbands who have spent years in jail, rather than give a get.[7] In one extreme case, the husband whose get was sought was already serving a fourteen-year jail sentence for statutory rape. Upon the wife's suit for a divorce, the court agreed that she was entitled to a get. The court reasoned that she was entitled to the get on the ground of "ma'us alay" (repulsiveness), since there was clear "amatla" (substantiation) that she had no ulterior motive in seeking the get. The court concluded that coercion by imprisonment was appropriate in such circumstances. However, what was the court to do, as the husband was already in jail? There was, therefore, no available remedy for the wife, and the court sadly concluded:[8]

> And now we turn to whom the matter is under their jurisdiction, to change the rule of compulsion with regard to those already in jail, to permit corporal punishment as in the Talmud, or solitary confinement or the like, so that the daughters of Israel not remain eternal widows.

Despite the above, there are many decisions of the Rabbinic courts that indicate great reluctance to force a husband to give a get, despite their power to do so. They have refused to accept the view of Maimonides, discussed above,[9] that a wife's claim that her husband's repulsiveness ("ma'us alay") prevents her from engaging in sexual relations with him entitles her to a get, unless a clear "amatla" exists, as in the above mentioned case.[10]

The courts have, however, sometimes utilized the ground of "ma'us alay," together with other grounds, to require a husband to give a get, especially where such "amatla" exists.[11] They have not limited the claim of "ma'us alay", where applicable, to instances of repugnance on the wife's part for sexual relations only, as would appear from a literal reading of Maimonides' view,[12] but have deemed it sufficient, when such claim is accepted, if she manifests hatred or intense dislike of her husband.[13]

On the other hand, in numerous decisions, some Israel courts have completely rejected the view of Maimonides regarding the wife's right to a get when she claims "ma'us alay", and have followed the view of Rabbenu Tam, discussed above,[14] that a husband may never be forced to give a get (except when obligated to do so under Talmudic law),[15] even where "amatla" for the wife's claim exists. They, in other instances, totally refrained from exercising compulsion, and have limited their intervention to recommending that the husband give a get.[16]

We see, therefore, that Israel courts, although sympathetic to the plight of the spouse who is unable to obtain a get, are nevertheless most cautious in utilizing their powers of coercion. The courts have not, as yet, arrived at a consistent position in this area of law. There is, however, a ray of hope that a solution to the problem may yet be found.

Although the Geonic takanah, which we discussed above,[17] has no binding authority in Israel, as elsewhere, there is an indication, in a recent decision of the Supreme Rabbinical Court,[18] of its continued viability, for some purposes at least. In that particular case, the court directed the husband to give his wife a get and stated that it would compel him to do so on various grounds, including the claim of "ma'us alay," as "amatla" for her claim existed, as well as on the basis of the Geonic takanah. In so holding, and *perhaps* reviving the takanah, at least when joined with other grounds justifying compulsion to give a get, the court stated:[19]

> But in the presented circumstances, her claim of "ma'us alay" is made manifest by the circumstances and we ourselves can establish that he is indeed repulsive to every normal woman on account of his mad behavior, as reflected in the District Court; we have no reason to suspect her (of making the claim of "ma'us alay") because she is a loose woman and seeks another. It is therefore appropriate in these circumstances to adhere to the Geonic takanah; and it may not be said that because (this takanah) has become annulled as reflected in the *Beth Yosef*[20] that it has totally lost all efficacy whatsoever. For it is reflected in . . . *Beth Yosef* that if the wife substantiates her claim of "ma'us alay," we force her husband to give a get. We therefore see that the takanah did not lose all efficacy, but as stated . . . , was annulled on condition that it could be re-enacted as and when desirable. This is so a *fortiori* in our case, where it is apparent to all that he is repulsive to her because of his madness, we may apply the takanah, according to all views of the matter.

The foregoing reflects, perhaps, that if a solution to the get problem is to be forthcoming in our generation, it will "come forth from Zion."

Part IV
FUTURE PROSPECTS:
LEGAL AND RABBINIC

Chapter XIV
LEGAL PROSPECTS

The material presented heretofore should have made it sufficiently clear to lawyer and layman alike that the failure to obtain a get may have tragic consequences to both parties to a marriage as well as to others, first and foremost to their children. It is therefore imperative that lawyers involved in divorce litigation and related get proceedings obtain a basic knowledge of the intricacies of Jewish law in this area.[1]

These considerations are not limited to religious, observant Jews. It may appear that, at the time of the civil divorce, neither party has any interest in obtaining a get. However, later developments may prove the failure to obtain a get to be most detrimental. There is always the possibility that either spouse may desire to remarry in a religious ceremony, and would be precluded from doing so because of the lack of a get. The opportunity to have arranged for a get, which may have existed at the time of the civil divorce, may later on be irretrievably lost.

In other instances, the failure to obtain a get may cause serious problems for the offspring of the wife's second marriage. Since without a get the first marriage is not dissolved, the wife's second marriage has no validity in the eyes of

Jewish law; indeed, it is considered adulterous and the children are deemed "mamzerim" (bastards), with all the serious disabilities attendant upon that status.

It is, therefore, important for the dedicated practitioner, in *every* case involving a civil divorce between Jewish spouses, to suggest to the parties the advisability of terminating the marriage religiously as well, by the giving and accepting of a get, preferably prior to the civil divorce.

It is not, of course, suggested that it remains the lawyer's duty to pursue the matter where the client is unwilling or uninterested. Nevertheless, a bit of foresight may avoid later grief.

There are various Rabbinical organizations which can provide further counseling and advice where necessary, and the lawyer would do well to acquaint himself with them and to refer his or her client to them, when advisable.[2]

If, however, it proves impossible to procure a get before the civil divorce, prudence will dictate that all efforts be made to obtain an agreement along the lines discussed in chapter XII above.

In view of the present trend of New York law, it is advisable to utilize an agreement to give a get wherever possible, despite the drawbacks in this approach discussed above.[3] This for the reason that there has been a greater degree of success with such type of agreement than with any other.

Thus, despite its drawbacks, such type of agreement, if obtained, is desirable on two grounds. The first is that the agreement itself, even in the absence of any attempt at court enforcement, may furnish a sufficient motive for the reluctant spouse to give or accept a get.

Secondly, if court enforcement becomes necessary, there is a good possibility that a court in New York will enforce the agreement under the cases discussed above. And, although the validity of a get so given under Jewish law is not without some residual doubt,[4] this approach appears to have been sanctioned, if not explicitly, then by silent acquiescence therein, by those Rabbinical authorities who have studied this problem.

An alternative approach is for the lawyer to attempt to obtain an agreement to submit the issue of the giving of a get to Rabbinical arbitration. The benefits of any such agreement are many, including enforceability by the civil courts under the decision of the Court of Appeals in *AVITZUR*, discussed above.[5] If the arbitration panel directs the giving of the get, there is substantial likelihood, although not a certainty, that such decision will be enforced by the civil courts under *AVITZUR*. It should be noted, however, that the Court of Appeals, in *AVITZUR*, did not render or even indicate any opinion as to the ultimate enforceability by the civil courts of a decision of the Rabbinic arbitrators directing the giving of a get. The Court of Appeals merely deferred such issues for later determination.

In addition, of course, this approach has the extra advantage that if the decision of the arbitration panel is enforced by the civil courts, any get so given would be valid under Jewish law, as discussed above.[6]

This is therefore an optimum approach which should be used where applicable, appropriate and possible.

If it is not possible to obtain any such agreement at all, the attorney is left to his legal ingenuity in attempting to obtain get relief for his client.

It may, in appropriate circumstances, be worthwhile to argue, as was done in the *STERN* and *MINKIN* cases discussed above,[7] that the traditional ketubah imparts an obligation to give a get. However, in view of the inherent weaknesses in this approach, it is suggested that it is properly avoided unless no other alternative exists.[8]

There may be other possible or potential remedies available if one spouse, out of malice, spite and ill-will refuses to give or accept a get. One of these is commencing action for damages. This approach is, however, the most tenuous, and the least likely to bear any legal fruition.[9]

In addition, it is important for the lawyer to keep abreast, if at all possible, of developments within the Jewish community in its ongoing attempts to deal with this problem from the point of view of Jewish law. There are several proposals presently under discussion, which, if adopted, will go a long way towards resolution of the problem, and the Matrimonial Bar would accordingly do well to remain attuned to the same.

As this book goes to press the New York Legislature has passed a bill which is now being presented for signature to Governor Mario Cuomo. This bill provides in substance that a final judgement of annulment or divorce will not be entered unless the party suing for the annulment or divorce (the plaintiff) has "taken all steps solely within his or her power to remove all barriers to the defendant's remarriage following the annulment or divorce."[10]

Assuming that the bill is signed into law by Governor Cuomo and that it withstands the constitutional attacks which are sure to come, it will be of great help in such cases where it is the party who is suing for the civil divorce who refuses to give or accept the get. This for the reason that in such circumstances he or she will be unable to obtain the civil divorce without first complying with the get procedures. But if, as frequently occurs, it is not the plaintiff but the defendant who is recalcitrant regarding his or her participation in get proceedings, the bill will have little effect, if any.

Chapter XV
RABBINIC PROPOSALS

There is no doubt but that the Rabbinate, in the past as well as at present, has evinced deep sympathy and concern for the "agunah," the "anchored" woman, who cannot remarry because she is unable to terminate her prior marriage by obtaining a get. This concern is reflected in the attempts to introduce a measure of equality in Jewish divorce law, discussed above,[1] as well as in continued attempts to date to resolve this problem.[2]

In the past twenty years, attempts to provide Rabbinic solutions to this problem have fallen into two distinct categories. The first category consists of solutions which, more or less, involve reapplications or revitalizations of concepts that have been rejected in the past, but which may merit further consideration.

Thus, one Rabbinic authority has again projected the concepts of conditional marriage,[3] similar to that proposed by the French Rabbis, which we have previously discussed.[4] In view, however, of the strenuous objection to that proposal in the past, it is not likely that it will achieve any greater acceptance in the future.

As an alternative, there remains the possible reinstatement

of the Geonic takanah, also discussed above,[5] in a modified form.

There is little doubt that the breakdown of Rabbinic and Geonic authority in Europe and elsewhere during the Middle Ages led to the rejection, at least in part, of the Geonic takanah. Under that takanah, a husband was forced by the Beth Din to give a get to his wife, whenever such was demanded by her. The power of the Geonim to do so was predicated upon the concept that all who marry do so in accordance with the will of the Rabbis. Thus, the Rabbis, in the exercise of their discretion, had authority to, in effect, annul the marriage as and when they saw fit and necessary. With the breakdown of Rabbinic and Geonic authority, and with the consequent delegation of legislative enactments of takanot to local Rabbinical courts, there was raised the horrid spectre that, if such a takanah was recognized by one local authority, it might not be recognized by local Rabbinical courts in other communities. The result would be that a marriage could be deemed terminated by divorce in one locality but not in other localities, with consequent hardships for both husband and wife.[6]

This writer has elsewhere suggested[7] that those historical realities which mandated, at least in part, the rejection of the Geonic takanah, may no longer be relevant as time goes on. In the State of Israel, for the first time in approximately 1600 years, the Jewish law of marriage and divorce is the law of the land. Thus today, at least in the State of Israel, objections regarding the local nature of any takanah to be enacted in the future may fall away.

This writer had further suggested, in 1977,[8] that a takanah similar to the Geonic one should be enacted in Israel today, fully applicable to residents of Israel over whom the Israel Rabbinical Courts exercise direct jurisdiction, albeit limited in scope as to non-residents. This will, of course, permit the courts to apply direct compulsion, as in Geonic times. On the other hand, if the husband or wife is obdurate in Israel, and refuses to give or accept a get, despite compulsion, or if the parties reside outside Israel and are hence not directly subject to the processes of the Rabbinic Courts in Israel, the Chief Rabbinate would, under any such takanah, be empowered or authorized to annul the marriage. The effect of such annulment would be to retroactively dissolve the marriage from the point of view of Jewish law, thereby eliminating the formal requirement of the giving of a get.[9]

It is conceded that this approach is quite radical in scope and concept, but its consideration is justified by the critical nature of the problem, and the human suffering caused by failure to resolve it.

It is interesting to note that this approach, advanced by the author in 1977, had previously been made in 1937, eleven years before the establishment of the State of Israel, by Rabbi M. Risikoff, who, in apparent anticipation of future events, made a similar suggestion.[10] He suggested vesting the Beth Din in Jerusalem with the power to, in effect, annul a marriage when a wife is unable to obtain a get. He suggested that, at the time of the wedding ceremony, the groom state:

> Thou are wedded unto me under the laws of Moses and Israel, and in accordance with the rules of the Beth Din Hagadol Hakavua (established) in Jerusalem.

Particularly instructive in this regard is the recent decision of the Supreme Rabbinical Court of Israel, discussed above.[11] In the portion of the decision quoted above,[12] Rabbi S. Goren, then Ashkenazi Chief Rabbi, and two other leading Israeli judges and scholars, Rabbis Y. Kafah and M. Eliahu, presently Sephardi Chief Rabbi, held that *there was* continuing validity to the Geonic takanah today, at least for some purposes, and indicated that such takanah could be reinstated.

It is suggested that such would indeed be appropriate and that prompt re-enactment is desirable.

The second category of projected solutions involves attempts by concerned Rabbis and Rabbinic bodies to provide prospective relief by means of a pre-marital agreement, whose purpose is to assure that every Jewish marriage which ends in civil divorce will henceforth be terminated religiously as well, by a get.

In so doing, the agreements under consideration attempt to avoid direct compulsion or coercion, thereby avoiding problems relating to a get given under compulsion. In addition, and by so avoiding direct compulsion or coercion, it is anticipated that these agreements will be enforceable in the secular courts, if necessary.

This general approach is, of course, not new, and has been attempted by the Conservative movement in its modification of the traditional ketubah.[13] One of the objections voiced by the Orthodox Rabbinate to the Conservative ketubah was that it lacked the requisites, under Jewish law, for a valid "kinyan" necessary to make a contract binding.[14] Most recently, Rabbi Judah Dick, a New York attorney, has suggested that this problem can be overcome by a written agreement pursuant to which each spouse, prior to the marriage, presently obligates himself and herself to pay the other a specified sum of money. These obligations are to be set forth in separate agreements which are absolute and unconditional. In addition, such agreements provide that these monetary obligations are waived or released upon the giving or acceptance of a get by one or the other spouse.[15]

They also contain an express waiver of the monetary obligations until such time as the civil courts shall have decided upon the legal dissolution of the marriage. Upon the obtaining of a civil divorce, the monetary obligations are effectuated, but they are released by the husband or the wife by the giving or acceptance of a get.

In addition, the documents contain a provision for Rabbinical arbitration of all disputes. A written explanation of the pre-nuptial agreement and accompanying documents is also provided for the parties.[16]

It is to be hoped that, in absence of a takanah of the type referred to above, such type of pre-nuptial agreement, or some modified version thereof, will find favor in the eyes of the Rabbinical authorities and gain swift implementation, and that any such type of agreement will also be found to be enforceable in the secular courts, if recourse to them is necessary.

A further suggestion which bears consideration in view of the decision of the Court of Appeals in *AVITZUR*, discussed above,[17] is that advanced by Rabbi Jechiel I. Perr.[18]

Rabbi Perr's suggestion, which has the approval of Rabbi Moshe Feinstein (a prominent living authority on Jewish law) conveyed to Rabbi Perr in a private communication, is that the parties should enter into a pre-nuptial agreement, not incorporated in the ketubah, pursuant to which they agree as follows:

> We, the undersigned, agree that if after we wed we, G-d forbid, separate, then each of us shall obey the order of a designated Beth Din regarding the giving or accepting of a get.

It is to be hoped that, failing to enact a takanah of the

type proposed above, the Rabbinic authorities will fashion a pre-nuptial agreement acceptable to the entire Jewish community.

There is now good reason to believe that any such type of pre-nuptial agreement will be enforced by the civil courts, if necessary. In view of the favorable prospect as to the enforceability of such agreements by the civil courts, the prompt implementation by the Rabbis of a pre-nuptial agreement of the types referred to above, or some modified version, is imperative.

EPILOGUE

The tragedy of spouses who are unable to obtain a get in order to terminate a dead marriage has been exacerbated in recent years by the rising divorce rate affecting all segments of our modern society.[1] As noted by the court in the case of *RUBIN v. RUBIN*:[2]

> With the sociological reality of a tremendously increased divorce rate upon us, a phenomenon which cuts across all levels of society, Orthodox Jews find themselves in matrimonial litigation more often and courts are called upon to weigh the import of ecclesiastical laws which are often made crucial by the contractual acts of the parties.[3]

It has been estimated that there are approximately 15,000 Orthodox Jewish women, in New York State alone, who are civilly divorced but are unable to obtain a get. They are hence unable to remarry under Jewish law,[4] and thus are forced to live in marital limbo.

This problem is further compounded by the instances, numbering in the hundreds and perhaps in the thousands, reported to the author and to other Rabbis and attorneys, of women who have been unable to obtain a get until they have complied with demands that have bordered upon extortion and blackmail. Clearly, the Jewish community as a whole, and the Orthodox Jewish community in particular, do not serve their best interests when permitting a situation which provides a breeding ground for greed to continue. Moreover, it is also quite clear that neither party ever really gains anything in the long run, when there is an ongoing battle over a get, *especially* when there are young and impressionable children involved. It is therefore most earnestly and emphatically recommended that *the giving or acceptance of a get should never be used as a weapon in divorce litigation.*

This is, of course, more easily written than effected, given the heated circumstances surrounding those embroiled in divorce litigation. And yet, the alternative is chaos for all concerned. It is quite apparent that it does neither the parties to the dispute, nor their children and relatives and indeed the Jewish community as a whole, any good to perpetually confront such problems.

This is not to say, however, that the Rabbis and Rabbinic leadership may abdicate their responsibility in this matter, but merely that the primary responsibility for eliminating the chaos in the community resulting from get litigation rests upon the parties themselves.

The first step towards any total resolution of this problem (which *must* ultimately come from Rabbinic action, including legislation of some sort), insofar as the parties themselves are concerned, must be to *stop utilizing the get as a club or bludgeon.*

The urgency of the problem is further made more manifest by the proliferation of late of groups of various kinds that are devoted to the alleviation of this problem. Let us make note of some of these groups.

1. *GET* (Getting Equitable Treatment) is an organization of Jewish men and women dedicated to assuring that a get is obtained whenever a marriage is dissolved by civil divorce. It utilizes persuasion and community pressure, if necessary, to encourage compliance with get procedures.

2. *AGUNAH* is a group organized by New York City Councilwoman Susan Alter, whose purpose is to provide support services and programs, including counseling, for women who are unable to obtain a get.

3. A major portion of the activities of the *Commission on Law and Public Affairs* (COLPA) involves participation in get litigation in the courts by the filing of briefs as *amicus curiae*, as was done in the *AVITZUR* case, discussed above.[5]

In addition, there have been numerous lectures and symposia conducted of late, as well as numerous articles in newspapers, magazines, and reviews, both general and legal, devoted to this issue.[6]

It requires no sociological expertise to assert that the alarming increase in the divorce rate, and consequent get problems, pose grave problems for the continued viability and stability of the Jewish family. It is therefore vital that more attention be paid within the Jewish community to those aspects of life relating to love, sex and marriage, as well as to the responsibilities of married life.

From the writer's professional experience with tens, if not hundreds, of women involved in get litigation, one common theme emerges. In the majority of instances there was a recurrent "courtship problem" which seems to have contributed to the end result of a dead marriage: the parties married without really having gotten to know each other. In the opinion of this author, it behooves the responsible authorities in the Jewish community to seriously study the get problem in all its ramifications, and to ascertain whether there is any correlation, particulary in the Orthodox Jewish community, between courtship patterns and the high incidence of divorce.

It is mandatory that the leaders of the Jewish community take the problem of the rising divorce rate seriously, and carefully evaluate all the potential solutions of the get problem.

The problems of the high divorce rate within the Jewish community, as well as of the recalcitrant spouse who refuses to give a get, are soluble and call for our best efforts to render them so.

NOTES

Chapter I

1. Mishnah, *Kiddushin*, 1:1, and Babylonian Talmud, *Kiddushin*, 2a, *et seq*.
2. B.T., *Kiddushin*, 2b; Maimonides, *Laws of Ishut*, chapt. 6, par. 1. See also, B.T., *Bava Batra*, 48b; *Shulḥan Arukh, Even Ha'ezer, Laws of Kiddushin*, chapt. 42.
3. Irwin H. Haut, *The Talmud as Law or Literature: An Analysis of David W. Halivni's Mekorot Umasorot* (Bet Sha'ar Press, New York, N.Y., 1982) p. 49, discussing the view of Prof. Halivni at *Mekorot Umasorot, Nashim* (D'vir, Tel Aviv, 1968) pp. 613-615.
4. B.T., *Kiddushin, Tosafot* 2b, s.v. "He prohibits her . . ."
5. 960-1028 C.E.
6. *Shulḥan Arukh, Even Ha'ezer, Laws of Kiddushin*, chapt. 27, par. 1. For other formal or ritual requirements of the marriage ceremony, see *ibid.*, chapt. 34; *Encyclopaedia Judaica*, s.v. "Marriage," pp. 1026, 1035-1042. For legal implications of this formula see chapt. III, *infra*.
7. *Shulḥan Arukh, Even Ha'ezer*, n.6, *ibid.*, chapts. 32-33.
8. See *Encyclopaedia Judaica*, n.6, *supra*, p. 1046.
9. For further discussion of distinction between "eirusin" and "nisuin" and legal consequences of such distinction, see *Encyclopaedia Judaica*, n.6, *supra*, pp. 1047-1050; *Shulḥan Arukh*, n.6, *supra*, chapts. 55-56, 61; *Encyclopedia Talmudit*,

s.v. "A'rusah" (Talmudic Encyclopedia Publ. Ltd., Jerusalem, 1976) p. 182 *et seq.*; B. Schereschewsky, *Family Law in Israel*, (Mass, Jerusalem, 1974, 2d ed., Hebrew) pp. 38-44. For discussion of various views as to whether "nisuin" is also effected by means other than those stated in text, as, e.g., by the appearance of the bride under the wedding canopy, see *Shulḥan Arukh, ibid.*, chapt. 55, par. 1, and, particularly, gloss of Isserles, and *Encyclopaedia Judaica, ibid.*, p. 1047.

10. Maimonides, *Laws of Ishut*, chapt. 15, pars. 19-20: "And the Rabbis ordained that a man should honor his wife more than himself, and he should love her as he does himself. If he has wealth he must provide for her according to his means. He may not terrorize her and his manner (conduct) with her must be with gentleness and he must be neither morose, nor harsh. And they have also commanded her that she should exceedingly honor her husband and she should be in awe of him and she should act in accordance with his wishes. He should be in her eyes as a lord or master, acting in accordance with his desires, and avoiding that which is repugnant to him . . ."

11. Schereschewsky, n. 9, *supra*, p. 105.

12. See chapter II, *infra*.

13. Schereschewsky, n. 9, *supra*, p.105.

14. *Ibid.*, p.106.

15. Mishnah, *Kiddushin*, 1:1. For extensive discussion of the legal effect of civil marriage under Jewish law, and as to whether a get is necessary in order to terminate the relationship, see Schereschewsky, n. 9, *supra*, pp. 83-95.

Chapter II

1. See chapter IX, *infra*.

2. See Schereschewsky, p. 98, n. 7, for further discussion, and particularly with respect to the effect of the Rule of Rabbenu Gershom, abrogating the right of a husband to divorce his wife against her will, upon requirement of ketubah. See also,

David Werner Amram, *The Jewish Law of Divorce*, (Hermon Press, New York, 1975) p. 114.

3. Maimonides, *Laws of Ishut*, chapt. 10, par. 10; *Shulḥan Arukh, Even Ha'ezer*, chapt. 66, pars 1-5; Amram, *ibid.*

4. For further discussion, see Schereschewsky, pp. 96-105; *Encyclopaedia Judaica*, s.v. "Ketubah," pp. 926-930.

5. For text of the ketubah, see Maimonides, *Laws of Yibbum and Ḥalitzah*, chapt. 4, par 33. The translation is taken, in part, from that of Rabbi Dr. Sidney Hoenig, in Levin and Kramer, *New Provisions in the Ketubah: A Legal Opinion*, (Yeshiva U., New York, 1955) p. 6, n. 13.

6. For discussion of the right of a wife to effect payment of the lien created by her ketubah from real property previously owned by her former husband, but which is now owned by third parties, see Amram, n. 2, *supra*, p. 113; Schereschewsky, pp. 236-244.

7. For a well-reasoned view that the right of a wife to collect her ketubah from "the best" of her husband's property influenced the English Law of Dower, see Jacob J. Rabinowitz, *Jewish Law: Its Influence on the Development of Legal Institutions*, (Bloch Publ. Co., New York, 1956) pp. 284-289.

8. Chapter I, *supra*.

9. For further discussion of this ritual in the context of the modification to the ketubah that was enacted by the Conservative Movement, to be discussed below at chapt. XI, see Lamm, "Recent Additions to the Ketubah, A Halakhic Critique," *Tradition*, vol. 2, no. 1, Fall 1959, pp. 93, 104.

10. *Shulḥan Arukh, Even Ha'ezer*, chapt. 115, par. 5; Schereschewsky, pp. 104-105.

11. Chapter II, *supra*.

12. The husband too could, by misconduct, acquire the title "mored," rebellious one. However, we limit our discussion to misconduct that effects loss of rights to the ketubah by the wife. For rules relating to the husband "mored," see Schereschewsky, pp. 180-185.

13. Mishnah, *Ketuboth* 7:6; *Shulḥan Arukh, Even Ha'ezer*, chapt. 115, par. 1; Amram, p. 123.
14. Mishnah, *Ketubot, ibid.; Shulḥan Arukh, ibid.*, par. 4; Amram, *ibid*.
15. *Shulḥan Arukh, ibid.*, par. 5.
16. *Shulḥan Arukh, Even Ha'ezer*, chapt. 117, pars. 4-10; Amram, pp. 122-123.
17. Chapter IX, *infra*.

Chapter III

1. See e.g., Mishnah, *Sanhedrin*, 1:1.
2. For an excellent, extensive discussion of the legislative authority of the Rabbis and takanot generally, see article "Takkanot," by Prof. M. Elon in *Encyclopaedia Judaica* vol. 15, p. 712.
3. B.T., *Gittin*, 33a.
4. For further discussion see M. Elon, *Ha-mishpat Ha'ivri* (Jerusalem: Magnes Press, 1973, Hebrew) vol. 2, pp. 518-527. Prof. Elon points out that the Rabbinic power to annul a valid marriage extended further, and even applied to situations wherein the rule that "all who marry are presumed to do so in consonance with the will of the Rabbis" was inapplicable, as e.g., B.T., *Bava Batra*, 48b, where equitable principles justify the annulment of the marriage.
5. For further on this point, including a discussion of the difference of opinion between Prof. M. Elon and Prof. D.W. Halivni about the nature of Rabbinic legislation, see Haut, *The Talmud as Law or Literature*, chapt. 5, and, particularly, pp. 72-73, ns. 14, 16.
6. See *ibid.*, for discussion of whether the phrase "would render nugatory the exercise of the court's power" originally formed a part of Rabbi Shimon's formulation of this rule.
7. B.T., *Gittin*, 33b. See also, Haut, n. 5, *supra*, pp. 74-75, ns. 23, 24.
8. B.T., *Gittin*, 33a.

Chapter IV

1. Deut. 24:1. "If a man takes a wife and lives with her. If she fails to please him because he finds something obnoxious about her and he writes her a bill of divorcement, hands it to her, and sends her away from his house . . ."
2. *Encyclopaedia Judaica,* p. 131, s.v. "Divorce."
3. B.T., *Bava Batra,* 167a, *et seq.*
4. For effect of the decree of Rabbenu Gershom on Talmudic law, see *infra,* chapter IX.
5. B.T., *Yevamot,* 112b.
6. Deut. 22:28-29.
7. Deut. 22:13-19.
8. Tanna who flourished in the second half of the First Century B.C.E., and first half of the First Century C.E.
9. B.T., *Gittin,* 90a.
10. Tanna who was a contemporary of Shammai.
11. N. 9, *supra.*
12. 50-135 C.E.
13. N. 9, *supra.* Compare rule prevailing in Western societies both ancient and modern. See *Corpus Juris* (American Law Book Co., London, 1920) vol. 19, p. 16, Sect. 2, "Divorce", where it is pointed out that, among the ancient Greeks and during the late Roman period, divorce was available with ease, and for slight cause. Among modern Western societies, apparently under the influence of Christianity: "The rule is universally accepted that a divorce will not be granted for a trivial reason, and will be granted only for reasons that are serious, weighty, grave and compelling, and which are recognized and sanctioned by law." (*Corpus Juris Secundum* [American Law Book Co., Brooklyn, New York] vol. 27A, p. 34. "Divorce").

    See also, *LIND v. LIND,* 452 N.Y.S. 2d 204, 206 (App. Div., 2d Dept., 1982):

    "Courts are loath to dissolve the bonds of matrimony for slight cause. Strained and even antagonistic relations between the parties do not alone justify judgment of separation (see *AVERETT v. AVERETT*, 189 App. Div. 250, 178 N.Y.S. 405, affd. 232 N.Y. 519, 134 N.E. 554). Mere allegations of cruel and inhuman treatment, without establishing a pattern of either physical violence or conditions rendering it unsafe for cohabitation, such as by presenting a threat to the health, safety or mental condition of the spouse, are insufficient (*RIOS v. RIOS*, 34 A.D. 2d 325, 311 N.Y.S. 2d 664, affd. 29 N.Y. 2d 840, 327 N.Y.S. 2d 853, 277 N.E. 2d 786). As the Court of Appeals recognized in *HESSEN v. HESSEN*, 33 N.Y. 2d 406, 411-412, 353 N.Y.S. 2d 421, 308 N.E. 2d 891, even a long and happy marital relationship may suffer the deleterious effects of the inevitable aging process on physical and mental disposition of the spouses, but that alone still would not constitute sufficient cruelty or inhumanity as to warrant dissolution of the marriage."

14. B.T., *Gittin*, 90b. See *Shulḥan Arukh, Even Ha'ezer*, chapt. 119, par. 1, and commentaries, *ad loc.*

15. Maimonides, *Laws of Divorce*, chapt. 2, par. 20: "we (exert) force upon him, until he says 'I am willing'," See Schereschewsky, pp. 318-319.

16. Schereschewsky, *ibid.*

17. Schereschewsky, pp. 274-275.

18. *Ibid.*, pp. 318-319.

19. See Maimonides, *Laws of Divorce*, chapt. 10, par. 23, and views of Ravad and *Maggid Mishneh, ad loc.* See also, *Shulḥan Arukh, Even Ha'ezer*, chapt. 119, par. 6 and commentaries. Amram, p. 46, n. 2, apparently errs in his understanding of Maimonides' view.

20. Maimonides, *ibid.*

21. Maimonides, *ibid.*, chapt. 2, par. 19, and commentaries *ad loc.*; *Shulḥan Arukh, Even Ha'Ezer, ibid.*, and chapt. 141, par. 6.

22. Chapter VI, *infra.*

23. See n. 13, *supra; Corpus Juris,* vol. 40, "Modern Civil Law" (1926), p. 1269, Sect. 38; *Corpus Juris*, vol. 19, "Divortium" (1920) p. 379.

24. For further discussion, see *Encyclopaedia Judaica*, s.v. "Divorce," p. 125; Schereschewsky, pp. 276-283.

Chapter V

1. Pp. 19-20, *supra*.
2. Maimonides, *Laws of Divorce*, chapt. 2, par. 20. See also, an excellent presentation of this view by Amram, pp.57-59.
3. B.T., *Gittin*, 88b; Maimonides, *ibid.*; *Shulḥan Arukh, Even Ha'ezer*, chapt. 134, par. 5. See generally, *Encyclopedia Talmudit*, vol. 5, s.v. "Get Me'useh," p. 698, n. 6. (Talmudic Encyclopedia, Publ. Ltd., Jerusalem, 1973).
4. *Encyclopedia Talmudit, ibid.*, p. 702, ns. 49-58.
5. For differing views, see *ibid.*, p. 701, ns. 36-46. But see particularly, Maimonides, n. 2, *supra*. See also, Haut, *The Talmud as Law or Literature*, p. 48.
6. B.T., *Gittin*, n. 3, *supra; Encylopedia Talmudit*, n. 3, *supra*, pp. 699-701, ns. 28-33; *Shulḥan Arukh, Even Ha'ezer*, chapt. 134, par. 9.
7. Chapter IX, *infra*.
8. B.T., *Ketubot*, 77a; *Shulḥan Arukh, Even Ha'ezer*, chapt. 154, pars. 1-2; Schereschewsky, pp. 285-288.
9. *Shulḥan Arukh, Even Ha'ezer, ibid.*, pars. 6-7; Schereschewsky, pp. 288-296.
10. Schereschewsky, pp. 296-298.
11. *Ibid.*, pp. 298-299.
12. Schereschewsky, p. 299.
13. B.T., *Ketubot*, n. 8, *supra*.
14. *Shulḥan Arukh, Even Ha'ezer*, chapt. 154, pars. 8-9. With respect to rules governing one spouse who wishes to go from the Diaspora to Israel, however, see *Shulḥan Arukh, ibid.*, chapt. 75, pars. 3-5.
15. See Karo, *Beth Yosef* on *Tur, Even Ha'ezer*, chapt. 134. Such was permitted on the basis that the Gentile courts were merely enforcing the decree of the Jewish courts, as discussed above in this chapter. But, for contrary view, see gloss of Isserles to *Shulḥan Arukh, Even Ha'ezer*, chapt. 154, par. 1. See also Amram, p. 75.

Chapter VI

1. See "form of get," chapter IV, *supra*.
2. *Encyclopedia Talmudit*, vol. 5, pp. 567, 626-627. See generally, *Shulḥan Arukh, Even Ha'ezer*, chapt. 127.
3. *Shulḥan Arukh, Even Ha'ezer*, chapt. 129. The proper orthography of personal and place names presents one of the primary concerns of the Rabbis who arrange gittin.
4. *Ibid.*, chapt. 128.
5. See "form of get," chapter IV, *supra*.
6. *Shulḥan Arukh, Even Ha'ezer*, chapt. 137, par. 1.
7. *Ibid.*, chapt. 143, par. 2.
8. N.6, *supra*.
9. View of Isserles and others, n. 6, *supra*. See Maimonides, *Laws of Divorce*, chapt. 8, par. 12. Maimonides rules likewise with respect to any type of condition which is not finite, e.g., "you are divorced on condition that you never drink wine." But, according to Maimonides, if the condition was of a finite duration, it is valid, even if the wife, as a practical matter, may die before the end of the stipulated period, as for example, "you are divorced on condition that you do not marry for fifty years." See also, *Shulḥan Arukh, Even Ha'ezer*, chapt. 143, par. 22.
10. Deut. 25:5-10.
11. See generally, B.T., *Yevamot; Encyclopedia Talmudit*, vol. 15, p. 615, *et seq*.
12. *Shulḥan Arukh, Even Ha'ezer*, chapt. 145, par. 2. See generally, *Shulḥan Arukh, Even Ha'ezer*, chapt. 143, par. 2.
13. *Shulḥan Arukh, Even Ha'ezer*, chapt. 144, par. 3.
14. See *Shulḥan Arukh, Even Ha'ezer*, chapt. 148, par. 20, and 149, par.1, *et seq*. Also see p. 44, *infra*. Even if there is no direct evidence of cohabitation, but two witnesses merely saw them secrete themselves together, the same rule applies and a second get is required.
15. *Shulḥan Arukh, Even Ha'ezer*, chapt. 130.

16. *Shulḥan Arukh, ibid.*, chapts. 138-140. See Haut, *The Talmud as Law or Literature*, pp. 45-47.
17. Amram, p.174.
18. *Shulḥan Arukh, Even Ha'ezer*, chapt. 139, pars. 2-3.
19. *Ibid.*, chapt. 140.

Chapter VII

1. B.T., *Kiddushin*, 6a.
2. The writer has basically followed the translation of David Werner Amram, as set forth in chapter 16 of the *Jewish Law of Divorce*. Some modifications and changes were made, however, where necessary or advisable. All paragraphs marked "Note" are glosses of Isserles, *ad loc.*
3. Gloss of Isserles, predicated upon the Talmudic statement quoted in text at n. 1, *supra.*
4. The reason for the rule of the removal of rings is that there should be a fulfillment of the requirement that the get be placed (or dropped) "in her hand" with nothing between her hand and the get, including any rings. See gloss of Isserles, *Shulḥan Arukh, Even Ha'ezer*, chapt. 139, par. 14.
5. To perform an act of "kinyan," or acquisition.
6. To ascertain if she is pregnant.
7. So as not to engender the suspicion of cohabitation and consequent invalidity of the get. See p. 30, *supra*, n. 14.

Chapter VIII

1. Leviticus 21:7. All Jews today are classified as being either "Kohanim", descendants of Aharon, brother of Moses, "Levi'im", descendants of Levi, or "Israelites", descendants of the tribes of Judah and Benjamin.
2. *Shulḥan Arukh, Even Ha'ezer*, chapt. 11.
3. *Ibid.*, chapt. 130, par. 21, gloss of Isserles. See also chapt. 12.

4. *Shulḥan Arukh, Even Ha'ezer,* chapt. 12.

5. *Ibid.,* chapt. 13.

6. Mishnah, *Moed Katan,* 1:7; *Shulḥan Arukh, Oraḥ Ḥayim,,* chapt. 546, par. 2.

7. *Ibid.* See Amram, pp. 81-82, who suggests that although "new" marriages are prohibited, the re-marriage of a divorced couple to each other is viewed, not as a "new" marriage, but as a continuation of the former marriage. The reason for this distinction, indicated by the Mishna, is that a new marriage is a source of great joy and it is thus inappropriate to confuse or combine such joy with the joy of the Festival, whereas, by implication, the re-marriage of a divorced couple is a source of lesser joy, and is, therefore, permitted on the Festival.

8. Deuteronomy 24:1-4. For further discussion, see Schereschewsky, p. 336, and Amram, pp. 82-84, who presents a speculative but interesting rationale for this rule.

9. Chapter II, *supra.*

10. *Ibid.* For further discussion, see Schereschewsky, pp. 337-338.

11. *Shulḥan Arukh, Even Ha'ezer,* chapt. 82, par. 6.; chapt. 90, par. 5 and commentaries ad loc.

12. *Ibid.,* chapt. 149, pars. 1-2. For further discussion, see Schereschewsky, pp. 341-342.

13. See *Shulḥan Arukh, Even Ha'ezer,* chapts. 71, 73. For further discussion with respect to the rights and obligations of parents in regard to their children during the subsistence of the marriage, including support obligations, see Schereschewsky, pp. 359-375.

14. *Shulḥan Arukh,* Even Ha'ezer, chapt. 82, par. 7.

15. *Ibid.*

16. *Shulḥan Arukh,* n. 14, *supra,* par. 7.

17. Isserles, *ibid.*

18. For further discussion and application of this concept in the context of cases involving custody disputes arising out of agreements to give a child a particular type of religious upbringing and education, see the following cases:

a-*PERLSTEIN* v. *PERLSTEIN*, 76 A.D. 2d 49, 429 N.Y.S. 2d 896 (1st Dept. 1980) (agreement to give child strictly religious education and upbringing upheld).

b-*GRUBER* v. *GRUBER*, 451 N.Y.S. 2d 117 (1st Dept. 1982) (agreement to give children yeshiva education upheld).

See also *FRIEDERWITZER* v. *FRIEDERWITZER*, 55 N.Y. 2d 89, 447 N.Y.S. 2d 893 (1982) and *SCHWARZMAN* v. *SCHWARZMAN*, 388 N.Y.S. 2d 993 (Sup. Ct., Nassau Co., 1976).

Chapter IX

1. Approximately 500 C.E.
2. Chapter III, *supra.*
3. P. 10, *supra.* That the Geonic takanah was predicated on their authority to annul a marriage is stated by Rabbenu Asher, *Responsa* (Grossman Publ. House, New York) no. 43, subd. 8.
4. *Ketubot,* 5:7.
5. B.T., *Ketubot,* 63b.
6. *Ibid.,* 64a.
7. B.T., *Ketubot,* 63b.
8. Tykocinski, C., *Tekanot Hageonim* (Sura, Jerusalem and Yesh. Univ., N.Y., 1960) chapt. 1. The author suggests that the takanah referred to by Sherira Gaon, who lived in the 10th Century C.E., may have been enacted as early as 651 C.E., but that it was probably enacted between 660-690; *ibid.,* p. 23.
9. For further discussion of this point see Haut, "A Problem in Jewish Divorce Law: An Analysis and Some Suggestions," *Tradition,* vol. 16, no. 3, Spring 1977, pp. 29,37, n. 59.
10. *Jewish Law Annual,* vol. 4, Mordechai A. Friedman, "Divorce Upon the Wife's Demand as Reflected in Manuscripts from the Cairo Geniza" (E.J. Brill, Leiden, 1981) p. 103. See also, Haut, "A Problem . . ." p. 37, ns. 53-55, for discussion of acceptance of Geonic takanah by Alfasi and others, including Rabbenu Gershom, and n. 28, *infra.*

11. Friedman, *ibid.*

12. 1135-1205 C.E.

13. *Laws of Ishuth*, chapt. 14, par. 14.

14. 1194-1270 C.E. *Ḥiddushei Ramban*, attributed to Rashba (Waxman and Reinman, New York, 1952) p. 110, s.v. "and we find."

15. 1250-1327 C.E. *Responsa*, no. 43, subd. 8.

16. 1100-1171 C.E. *Sefer Hayashar* (Shai Publications, 1959), Sect. 599.

17. For further discussion of the views of Maimonides, Rabbenu Asher, Naḥmanides, and for critique of Rabbenu Tam, see Haut, n. 9, *supra*, pp. 37-40. See also chapter XV, *infra*.

18. Text in n. 7, *supra*.

19. 1030-1105 C.E.

20. Rashi, B.T., *Ketubot*, 63b, s.v. "we do not force her." See Maimonides, *Laws of Ishuth*, chapt. 14, par. 8; Rashbam, quoted by *Shiltay Ha'gibborim* on *Alfasi, ad loc.*

21. *Laws of Ishuth, ibid.*

22. See Haut, n. 9, *supra*, p. 45, n. 34, and *infra*, at p. 87.

23. N.15, *supra*.

24. N.16, *supra*; Tur, *Even Ha'ezer*, chapt. 77 and Karo, *Beth Yosef, ad loc; Shulḥan Arukh, Even Ha'ezer*, chapt. 77, pars. 2-3, and view of Isserles, par. 3; Tosafot, *Ketubot*, 63b-64a, s.v. "but if she says."

25. *Hagahot Maimuniyot*, Maimonides, *Laws of Ishut*, chapt. 14, par. 8, subd. 5: "We don't accept her claim (of repulsiveness) unless she gives a substantiation to her claim, which appears plausible to the sages of the place as to why she is unable to stand him ('ma'us alay'), that she would otherwise remain with him except for this matter that she claims causes him to be repulsive to her."

26. For further discussion of the views of Maimonides, Rabbenu Asher, Rabbenu Tam, and the attempted compromise between the differing views sought by the authority cited in n. 25, *ibid.*, see Haut, n. 9, *supra*, pp. 33-35 and, particularly, p. 45, n. 40. See also, p. 96, *infra*, for critique of Rabbenu Tam's view.

27. See S. Eidelberg, *Teshuvot Rabbenu Gershom Meor Hagolah* (Yesh. Univ., 1956), pp. 19-21. Rabbenu Gershom lived in Mayence; he was born in 960 and died in 1028. For extensive discussion of whether he did, in fact, promulgate this takanah, which has been attributed to him, see, *Encyclopaedia Judaica* pp. 511, 512, s.v. "Gershom Ben Judah Me'or Hagolah"; A. Grossman, *The Early Sages of Ashkenaz* (Magnes Press, Jerusalem, 1981, Hebrew) chapt. 3, and, particularly, p. 145, ns. 135-137, and p. 147, n. 143. See also, Rabbenu Asher, *Responsa*, n.15, *supra*, who states: " . . . there was a sage in our country (Germany) whose name was Rabbenu Gershom, who enacted great tekanot in areas of divorce and he lived in the period of the Geonim, and his tekanot and decrees were established as if given at Sinai by virtue of their widespread acceptance . . ."

28. Eidelberg, n. 27, *ibid.*, sect. 40, pp. 110-112; *Hagahot Harosh, Ketubot*, sect. 35, p. 246; Grossman, n. 27, *ibid.*, p. 148, n. 146.

29. See Grossman, n. 27, *supra*, at p. 148.

30. *Responsa*, n. 15, *supra*, no. 42, subd. 1.

31. See Grossman, n. 27, *supra*, for discussion as to whether this takanah, as with the takanah of Rabbenu Gershom discussed previously, is properly attributed to him. For the scope, duration, effect and degree of acceptance of the takanah prohibiting polygamy see, *Shulḥan Arukh, Even Ha'ezer*, chapt. 1, par. 10, and extensive gloss of Isserles, *ad loc.;* Schereschewsky, 67-80.

32. *Shulḥan Arukh, ibid.*, and, particularly, view of Isserles, *ad loc.*

33. *Shulḥan Arukh, Even Ha'ezer*, n. 31, *supra*, and commentaries *ad loc.; Shulḥan Arukh, ibid.*, chapt. 115, par. 4, and view of Isserles, *ad loc.* See also, Schereschewsky, pp. 78-80, with respect to rule requiring consent of one hundred rabbis, and pp. 273-274. For discussion of differing views as to whether consent of one hundred Rabbis is necessary when the wife is otherwise obligated by law to accept a get, as where she is a "moredet," or whether only a decree of a Beth

Din is necessary, see Schereschewsky, 77, and p. 324, n. 37. See also, p. 85, *infra*, n. 3.

34. Schereschewsky, pp. 325-326.

Chapter X

1. *Corpus Juris*, vol. 40, "Modern Civil Law," p. 1269, n. 17.
2. *Ibid.*, ns. 17-19.
3. *Ibid.*, ns. 19-20.
4. *Corpus Juris*, vol. 19, "Divortium," p. 379, n. 10.
5. *Ibid.*
6. A. Freimann, *Seder Kiddushin Ve'nisuin* (Mossad Harav Kook, Jerusalem, 1964), pp. 388-389. For an excellent and complete historical survey of this area of law see Freimann, *ibid.*, at pp. 385-397. See also, M. Meiselman, *Jewish Woman in Jewish Law* (Ktav Publ. House, Yesh. Univ. Press, New York, 1978), chapt. 17.
7. Freimann, *ibid.*
8. Freimann, n. 6, *supra.*
9. Freimann, n. 6, *supra*, at p. 390.
10. Freimann, n. 6, *supra*, pp. 390-394.
11. See p. 30, *supra.*
12. Epstein, *Hatza'ah L'ma'an Takanat Agunot* (New York, 1930). See also, by the same author, *L'sheilat Ha'agunah* (New York, 1940).
13. In all fairness to Rabbi Epstein, it must be pointed out that he specifically addressed the objection to his proposal referred to in the text. See *L'sheilat Ha'aguna*, n. 12, *ibid.* and, particularly, pp. 151-176. Meiselman, n. 6, *supra*, is thus in error when he suggests, at p. 107, that Rabbi Epstein ignored such objection. For further discussion of the effect of cohabitation on the validity of a get, see pp. 29-30, 44, *supra.*

Chapter XI

1. Quoted from A. Leo Levin and Meyer Kramer, *New Provisions in the Ketubah: A Legal Opinion* (Yesh. Univ., 1955), p. 2.
2. *Ibid.*
3. Lamm, "Recent Additions to the Ketubah, A Halakhic Critique," *Tradition*, vol. 2, no. 1, Fall 1959, p. 93.

Chapter XII

1. 16 D. and C. 290 (Court of Common Pleas, Phila., Pa., 1931).
2. 138 N.Y.S. 2d 366 (Sup. Ct., Queens Co., 1954).
3. *Ibid.*, at p. 373.
4. 3 A.D. 2d 853, 161 N.Y.S. 2d 694 (2d Dept., 1957).
5. 90 Misc. 2d 784, 395 N.Y.S. 2d 877 (Sup. Ct., Kings Co., 1976).
6. 57 A.D. 2d 863, 394 N.Y.S. 2d 253 (2d Dept., 1977).
7. See lower court decision, 395 N.Y.S. 2d 880, where the court states: "Defendant urges as an affirmative defense that plaintiff violated this paragraph by vacating the marital premises without obtaining a "Get," thus waiving her right to the "Get." The court rejects this argument. It is the defendant who refuses to give the plaintiff a "Get" in violation of the agreement. Defendant should not thereby benefit because the plaintiff chose to comply with another provision of the agreement requiring her to vacate the marital premises on or before April 1, 1974."
8. 75 Misc. 2d 776, 348 N.Y.S. 2d 61 (Family Court, Bronx Co., 1973).
9. Chapter IV, *supra*.
10. N. 8, *supra*, at pp. 65-66.
11. N. 8, *supra*, at p. 67.

12. *New York Law Journal,* May 4, 1978 (Sup. Ct., N.Y. Co., Blyn, J., p. 7, Col. 2).
13. The author is informed that the get was given by the husband shortly after Justice Blyn's decision.
14. 42 A.D. 2d 517, 344 N.Y.S. 2d 482 (1st Dept., 1973).
15. N.14, *ibid.,* at pp. 484-485.
16. See, however, a recent unreported decision of the Court of Appeals of Ohio, County of Cuyohoga, in the case of *STEINBERG v. STEINBERG,* no. 44125, decided 6-24-82, supplied by courtesy of Harry M. Brown Esq. of Cleveland Ohio, in which the Court refused to enforce an agreement to give a get under provisions of the Ohio Constitution.
17. Chapter XIV, *infra.*
18. See majority and dissenting opinions in *MARGULIES v. MARGULIES,* n. 14, *supra; RUBIN v. RUBIN,* n. 8, *supra.*
19. P. 24, *supra.*
20. 45 A.D. 2d 738, 356 N.Y.S. 2d 672 (2d Dept., 1974).
21. *Ibid.,* p. 673.
22. N. 14, *supra.*
23. 449 N.Y.S. 2d 83 (3d Dept., 1982).
24. Quoted from an unreported decision of lower court by Justice Klein, contained in record on appeal, p. 6.
25. *Ibid.*
26. N.24, *supra,* at p. 8.
27. N. 23, *supra.*
28. N. 23, *supra,* at p. 84.
29. *Ibid.*
30. 58 N.Y. 2d 108, 459 N.Y.S. 2d 572 (1983). For full text of decision of Court of Appeals, see Appendix B.
31. Chapt. 2, *supra.*
32. *MORRIS v. MORRIS,* 36 D.L.R. 3d 447 (Manitoba, Q.B., 1973).
33. 42 D.L.R. 3d 550 (Manitoba Ct. App., 1973).
34. *New York Law Journal,* Aug. 8, 1979 (Sup. Ct., Kings Co., p. 13, col. 5).
35. 180 N.J. Super. 260, 434 A. 2d 666 (1981).

36. 442 N.Y.S. 2d 928 (Sup. Ct., Kings Co., 1981) *aff'd* 449 N.Y.S. 2d 806 (2d Dept., 1982). Motion for leave to appeal to the Court of Appeals denied.
37. 442 N.Y.S. 2d at 931.
38. N. 36, *supra*.

Chapter XIII

1. Falk, *The Divorce Action by the Wife in Jewish Law* (Institute for Legislative Research and Comparative Law, Jerusalem, 1973) p. 32; *Encyclopaedia Judaica*, s.v. "Divorce." pp. 122, 134-135.
2. Falk, *ibid*.
3. P. 56, *supra*, n. 33. For an extensive discussion of this point, see *Piskei Din*, vol. 10, pp. 168, 179 (Supreme Rabbinical Court, Jerusalem, 1976). See also, *Piskei Din*, vol. 11, pp. 275, 279 (Haifa Rabbinical District Court, 1980).
4. *Ibid*.
5. Pp. 19-20, *supra*.
6. *Ibid*.
7. Falk, n. 1, *supra*, pp. 41-42.
8. *Piskei Din*, vol. 8, pp. 124, 128 (Haifa Rabbinical District Court, 1970). See also, *Piskei Din*, vol. 11, p. 300 (Tel Aviv-Jaffa Rabbinical District Court, 1978), where the husband from whom a get was sought was in jail because of various offenses. The issue presented was whether, in those circumstances wherein Jewish law did not permit compulsion to force a husband to give a get, a Beth Din could properly intercede with prison authorities to reduce his sentence if he gave his wife a get, or whether even such would yet constitute duress sufficient to invalidate the get, if given.
9. P. 53, *supra*.
10. Text, at n. 8, *supra*. See also, with respect to substantiation (*amatla*) requirements, p. 54, n. 25, *supra*.
11. *Piskei Din*, vol. 3, p. 3 (Supreme Rabbinical Court, Jerusalem, 1955); *Piskei Din*, vol. 5, p. 154 (Haifa Rabbinical District

Court, 1964); *Piskei Din*, vol. 9, p. 171 (Tel Aviv–Jaffa Rabbinical District Court, 1973); *Piskei Din*, vol. 12, p. 3 (Supreme Rabbinical Court, Jerusalem, 1981).

12. N. 9, *supra*.
13. *Piskei Din*, vol. 9, pp. 171, 182, n. 11, *supra; Piskei Din*, vol. 5, pp. 154, 157, n. 11, *supra; Piskei Din*, vol. 8, pp. 124, 126, n. 8, *supra*.
14. P. 54, *supra*.
15. See pp. 24-25, *supra*.
16. *Piskei Din*, vol. 9, p. 94 (Supreme Rabbinical Court, Jerusalem, 1973); *Piskei Din*, vol. 7, pp. 201, 204 (Supreme Rabbinical Court, Jerusalem, 1968); *Piskei Din*, vol. 7, p. 3 (Supreme Rabbinical Court, Jerusalem, 1967). For further discussion, see Haut, *Tradition*, Appendix, pp. 41-42.
17. Pp. 51-52, *supra*.
18. *Piskei Din*, vol. 12, p. 3, n. 11, *supra*.
19. *Ibid.*, pp. 9-10.
20. Law compendium written by Yosef Karo as commentary on *Arba'ah Turim*.

Chapter XIV

1. See Haut, "Not Getting a 'Get' Can be a Jewish Family Law Problem," *New York Law Journal*, 8/17/81, p. 1, col. 2.
2. See Haut, n. 1, *supra*, p. 6, col. 1.
3. P. 75, *supra*.
4. *Ibid*.
5. Pp. 79-80, *supra*.
6. P. 76, *supra*.
7. Pp. 81-82, *supra*.
8. But see, S. Friedell, "The First Amendment and Jewish Divorce: A Comment on *STERN v. STERN*," *Journal of Family Law*, vol. 18, p. 525.
9. But see, Haut, n. 1, *supra*, p. 6, col. 3, n. 28; Friedell, *ibid.*, pp. 532-533, ns. 20-21. See also, *CARTER v. ANDRIANI*, 443 N.Y.S. 2d 157 (1st Dept., 1981), permitting recovery of money damages for intentional infliction of emotional distress.
10. See Senate Bill no. S.6647, Assembly Bill no. A.6423, sponsored by Senator Martin Connor and Assemblyman Sheldon Silver (passed May 25, 1983). The bill also provides that in uncontested proceedings for annulment or divorce a final judgment shall not be entered unless each party "has taken all

steps solely within his or her power to remove all barriers to the other party's remarriage following the annulment or divorce."

Chapter XV

1. Chapter IX.
2. See chapters X, XI, *supra*. For historical survey of such attempts from approximately 1300 C.E. to the modern period, see A. Freimann, *Seder Kiddushin Ve'nisuin*, pp. 385-397.
3. E. Berkovits, *T'nai B'nisuin U'vget* (Mossad Harav Kook, Jerusalem, 1967). For further discussion, see B. Greenberg, *On Women and Judaism* (Jewish Publ. Soc. of America, Phila. Pa., 1981), pp. 136-138. For critique of Berkovits' view, see Kasher, "In the matter of T'nai B'nisuin," *Noam*, vol. 12, p. 338.
4. Chapter X,*supra*.
5. Chapter IX, *supra*.
6. For further discussion of this point see an excellent article by M. Elon, in *Encyclopaedia Judaica*, s.v. "Takkanot," pp. 712, 723-724.
7. See Haut, *Tradition*, pp. 38-39.
8. *Ibid*.
9. See Haut, *Tradition*, p. 40, n. 69, for a discussion of the view that annulment of marriage may eliminate the need for a get.
10. Freimann, p. 393.
11. Pp. 87-88, *supra*.
12. P. 88, *supra*.
13. Chapter XI, *supra*.
14. P. 65, *supra*, n.3.
15. See Judah Dick, "Is an Agreement to Deliver or Accept a *Get* in the Event of a Civil Divorce Halachically Feasible?" (*Tradition,* Summer 1983).
16. For a similar proposal, which may, however, fail the test of enforceability in the civil courts, if such should be necessary, by reason of rules relating to waiver, see J.D. Bleich, "Modern-Day Agunot, A Proposed Remedy," *Jewish Law Annual*, vol. 4, p. 167 (E.J. Brill, Leiden, 1981) and *KATZENSTEIN v. KATZENSTEIN*, 455 N.Y.S. 2d 100 (2d Dept., 1982).
17. Pp. 79-80, *supra*.
18. *Jewish Observer*, October 1982.

Epilogue

1. See *New York Times*, 11/13/81, p. A 12, col. 1, "Texas Cities Lead U.S. in the Rate of Divorce." The study reflects the growing rate of divorce in the U.S. as follows:

DIVORCES IN THE U.S.

Number per 1,000 population in the Census Bureau's 25 largest Standard Metropolitan Statistical Areas

	1979	'76	'70
Dallas-Ft. Worth	8.2	7.7	6.5
Houston	8.2	7.4	5.5
Tampa-St. Petersburg	8.1	7.2	5.0
Miami	7.3	7.3	5.6
Seattle	6.9	7.4	5.6
Atlanta	6.9	6.9	4.5
Anaheim	6.8	6.8	6.1
San Francisco	6.2	6.3	5.6
Denver	6.1	7.1	5.3
Riverside-San Bernardino	6.1	6.0	5.1
San Diego	6.0	6.8	5.9
Los Angeles-Long Beach	5.4	5.8	5.8
St. Louis	5.1	4.9	3.5
Cleveland	4.9	5.0	3.6
District of Columbia	4.7	4.1	2.3
Detroit	4.6	4.6	3.4
Minneapolis-St. Paul	4.4	N.A.	2.8
Baltimore	4.3	4.1	2.6
Chicago	4.1	4.2	3.0
New York	3.7	2.8	1.3
Philadelphia	3.4	2.9	1.8
Pittsburgh	3.2	3.2	1.9
Nassau-Suffolk	3.0	2.3	0.5
Newark	3.0	2.8	1.4
Boston	2.8	2.8	1.7

Source: National Center for Health Statistics

2. Discussed at pp. 70-73, *supra*.
3. 348 N.Y.S. 2d, p. 63.
4. See *New York Times*, 7/5/82, p. 40, col. 2, "Orthodox Jewish Divorce: The Religious Dilemma." In the text of the article, the figure of *150,000* is given for the number of Jewish women, in New York State alone, who are unable to obtain a get. This is obviously a misprint.
5. Pp. 79-80, *supra*.
6. For a selected bibliography on the enforcement of Jewish divorce in secular courts, supplied by courtesy of Prof. Dov Frimer of Touro Law School, see APPENDIX A.

Appendix A
BIBLIOGRAPHY

GENERAL BIBLIOGRAPHY
OF SECONDARY SOURCES CITED

1. Amram, David Werner, *The Jewish Law of Divorce* (New York: Hermon Press, 1975)
2. Berkovitz, E., *T'nai B'nisuin U'vget* (Jerusalem: Mossad Harav Kook, 1967, Hebrew)
3. Eidelberg, S., *Teshuvot Rabbenu Gershom Meor Hagolah* (Yesh. U., 1956)
4. Elon, Menaḥem, *Ha-Mishpat Ha'Ivri* (Jerusalem: Magnes Press, 1973)
5. Epstein, L., *Hatza'ah L'maan Takanat Agunot* (Monograph, New York, 1930)
6. Epstein, L., *L'sheilat Ha'agunah* (New York, 1940)
7. Falk, Z., *The Divorce Action by the Wife in Jewish Law* (Jerusalem: Institute for Legislative Research and Comparative Law, 1973, Hebrew)
8. Freimann, A., *Seder Kiddushin Ve'nisuin* (Jerusalem: Mossad Harav Kook, 1964, Hebrew)
9. Greenberg, Blu, *On Women and Judaism* (Philadelphia: Jewish Publication Society of America, 1981)
10. Grossman, A., *The Early Sages of Ashkenaz* (Jerusalem: Magnes Press, 1981, Hebrew)
11. Haut, Irwin H., *The Talmud as Law or Literature: An Analysis of D.W. Halivni's Mekorot Umasorot* (New York: Bet Sha'ar Press, 1982)

12. Kasher, M., "In the Matter of T'nai B'nisuin," *Noam*, vol. 12, p. 338 (Hebrew)
13. Lamm, Norman, "Recent Additions to the Ketubah, A Halakhic Critique" *Tradition*, vol.2, no.1, Fall 1959, p.93
14. Meiselman, M., *Jewish Woman in Jewish Law* (New York: Ktav Publishing House, Yesh. U. Press, 1978)
15. Rabinowitz, Jacob J., *Jewish Law: Its Influence on the Development of Legal Institutions* (New York: Bloch Publ. Co., 1956)
16. Schereschewsky, B., *Family Law in Israel* (Jerusalem: Rubin Mass., 1974, 2d. Ed., Hebrew)
17. Tykocinski, C., *Tekanot Hageonim* (Jerusalem: Sura and Yesh. U., 1960, Hebrew)

ON THE ENFORCEMENT OF
JEWISH DIVORCE IN SECULAR COURTS

1. Frank A. Baron, "Treatment of Jewish Law in American Decisions," 9 *Israel Law Review* 85-96 (1974)
2. G.W. Bartholomew, "Application of Jewish Law in England" 3 *Malaya Law Review* 83-111 (1961)
3. J. David Bleich, *Contemporary Halakhic Problems* (New York: Ktav Publishing House, 1977) pp. 154-159
4. J. David Bleich, *New York Law Journal*, July 5, 1974 (p. 4, col. 8)
5. Comment "Jewish Divorce and the Civil Law," 12 *De Paul Law Review* 295-305 (1963)
6. David Ellenson and James S. Ellenson, "American Courts and the Enforceability of a *Ketubah*," *Conservative Judaism*, vol. 35, no. 3 Spring, 1982, pp. 35-42
7. Steven F. Friedell, "Enforceability of Religious Law in Secular Courts—It's Kosher but is it Constitutional?" 71 *Michigan Law Review* 1641 (1973)
8. Steven F. Friedell, "The First Amendment and Jewish Divorce: A Comment on *STERN v. STERN*," 18 *Journal of Family Law* 525-535 (1980)

9. H. Patrick Glenn, "Where Heavens Meet: The Compelling of Religious Divorces," 28 *The American Journal of Comparative Law* 1-38 (1980)

10. M.D. Gouldman, "The Recalcitrant Husband," 3 *Israel Law Review* 315-319 (1968)

11. Irwin H. Haut, "A Problem in Jewish Divorce Law: An Analysis and Some Suggestions," *Tradition*, vol. 16, no. 3, Spring 1977, pp. 29-49

12. Irwin H. Haut, "Not Getting a 'Get' Can Be a Jewish Family Law Problem," *New York Law Journal*, August 17, 1981 (p. 1, col. 2)

13. Joseph Keller, *New York Law Journal*, March 22, 1982 (p. 2)

14. A. Leo Levin and Meyer Kramer, *New Provisions in the Ketubah: A Legal Opinion* (Monograph, Yesh. U., 1955)

15. J.D.M. Lew, "Jewish Divorces," 123 *New Law Journal* 829-830 (1973)

16. Susan Mardment, "Legal Effect of Religious Divorces" 37 *Modern Law Review* 611-626 (1974)

17. Bernard J. Meislin, "Civil Court Enforcement of Agreement to Obtain a 'Get'," 1 *The Jewish Law Annual* 224-227 (1978)

18. Bernard J. Meislin, *Jewish Law in American Tribunals* (New York: Ktav Publishing House, 1976), pp. 71-95

19. Bernard J. Meislin, "Varia Americana: Divorce," 2 *The Jewish Law Annual* 217-218 (1979)

20. E. Mickleioright, "Jewish Problems and an Ecclesiastical Judge," 123 *New Law Journal* 1147-1149 (1973)

21. Abraham J. Multer, *New York Law Journal*, April 1, 1982 (p. 2)

22. Emanuel Rackman, *New York Law Journal*, March 18, 1982 (p. 2)

23. Martha J. Schechter, "Civil Enforcement of Jewish Marriage Contract," 9 *Journal of Family Law* 425-432 (1970)

24. Martha Schechter, "Enforceability of Religious Law in Secular Courts—It's Kosher but is it Constitutional?", 71 *Michigan Law Review.*, 1641 (1973)

25. See also *Jewish Law Annual*, Volume 4 (1981)

Appendix B

OPINION

3   No. 5
Susan R. Avitzur, Appelant,
v.
Boaz Avitzur, Respondent.

WACHTLER, J.

This appeal presents for our consideration the question of the proper role of the civil courts in deciding a matter touching upon religious concerns. At issue is the enforceability of the terms of a document, known as a Ketubah, which was entered into as part of the religious marriage ceremony in this case. The Appellate Division held this to be a religious covenant beyond the jurisdiction of the civil courts. However, we find nothing in law or public policy to prevent judicial recognition and enforcement of the secular terms of such an agreement. There should be a reversal.

Plaintiff and defendant were married on May 22, 1966 in a ceremony conducted in accordance with Jewish tradition. Prior to

133

the marriage ceremony, the parties signed both a Hebrew/Aramaic and an English version of the "Ketubah". According to the English translation, the Ketubah evidences both the bridegroom's intention to cherish and provide for his wife as required by religious law and tradition and the bride's willingness to carry out her obligations to her husband in faithfulness and affection according to Jewish law and tradition. By signing the Ketubah, the parties declared their "desire to *** live in accordance with the Jewish law of marriage throughout [their] lifetime" and further agreed as follows:

> "We, the bride and bridegroom *** hereby agree to recognize the Beth Din of the Rabbinical Assembly and the Jewish Theological Seminary of America or its duly appointed representatives, as having authority to counsel us in the light of Jewish tradition which requires husband and wife to give each other complete love and devotion, and to summon either party at the request of the other, in order to enable the party so requesting to live in accordance with the standards of the Jewish law of marriage throughout his or her lifetime. We authorize the Beth Din to impose such terms of compensation as it may see fit for failure to respond to its summons or to carry out its decision."

Defendant husband was granted a civil divorce upon the ground of cruel and inhuman treatment on May 16, 1978. Notwithstanding this civil divorce, plaintiff wife is not considered divorced and may not remarry pursuant to Jewish law, until such time as a Jewish divorce decree, known as a "Get", is granted. In order that a Get may be obtained plaintiff and defendant must appear before a "Beth Din", a rabbinical tribunal having authority to advise and pass upon matters of traditional Jewish law. Plaintiff sought to summon defendant before the Beth Din pursuant to the provision of the Ketubah recognizing that body as having authority to counsel the couple in the matters concerning their marriage.

Defendant has refused to appear before the Beth Din, thus preventing plaintiff from obtaining a religious divorce. Plaintiff brought this action, alleging that the Ketubah constitutes a marital contract, which defendant has breached by refusing to appear before the Beth Din, and she seeks relief both in the form of a declaration to that effect and an order compelling defendant's specific performance of the Ketubah's requirement that he appear before the Beth Din. Defendant moved to dismiss the complaint upon the grounds that the court lacked subject matter jurisdiction and the complaint failed to state a cause of action, arguing that resolution of the dispute and any grant of relief to plaintiff would involve the civil court in impermissible consideration of a purely religious matter. Plaintiff, in addition to opposing the motion, cross-moved for summary judgment.

Special Term denied defendant's motion to dismiss, noting that plaintiff sought only to compel defendant to submit to the jurisdiction of the Beth Din, an act which plaintiff had alleged defendant bound himself to do. That being the only object of the lawsuit, Special Term was apparently of the view that the relief sought could be granted without impermissible judicial entanglement in any doctrinal issue. The court also denied plaintiff's motion for summary judgment, concluding that issues concerning the translation, meaning and effect of the Ketubah raised factual questions requiring a plenary trial.

The Appellate Division modified, granting defendant's motion to dismiss. Inasmuch as the Ketubah was entered into as part of a religious ceremony and was executed, by its own terms, in accordance with Jewish law, the court concluded that the document constitutes a liturgical agreement. The Appellate Division held such agreements to be unenforceable where the State, having granted a civil divorce to the parties, has no further interest in their marital status.

Accepting plaintiff's allegations as true, as we must in context of this motion to dismiss, it appears that plaintiff and defendant, in signing the Ketubah, entered into a contract which formed the basis for their marriage. Plaintiff has alleged that, pursuant to the terms of this marital contract, defendant promised that he would, at plaintiff's request, appear before the Beth Din for the purpose of allowing that tribunal to advise and counsel the parties in matters concerning their marriage, including the granting of a Get. It should be noted that plaintiff is not attempting to compel defendant to obtain a Get or to enforce a religious practice arising solely out of principles of religious law. She merely seeks to enforce an agreement made by defendant to appear before and accept the decision of a designated tribunal.

Viewed in this manner, the provisions of the Ketubah relied upon by plaintiff constitute nothing more than an agreement to refer the matter of a religious divorce to a nonjudicial forum. Thus, the contractual obligation plaintiff seeks to enforce is closely analogous to an antenuptial agreement to arbitrate a dispute in accordance with the law and tradition chosen by the parties. There can be little doubt that a duly executed antenuptial agreement, by which the parties agree in advance of the marriage to the resolution of disputes that may arise after its termination, is valid and enforceable (e.g., *Matter of Sunshine*, 40 NY2d 875, affg 51AD2d 326; *Matter of Davis*, 20 NY2d 70). Similarly, an agreement to refer a matter concerning marriage to arbitration suffers no inherent invalidity (*Hirsch v Hirsch*, 37 NY2d 312; see *Bowmer v Bowmer*, 50 NY2d 288, 293). This agreement—the Ketubah— should ordinarily be entitled to no less dignity than any other civil contract to submit a dispute to a nonjudicial forum, so long as its enforcement violates neither the law nor the public policy of this State (*Hirsch v Hirsch, supra*, at p 315).

Defendant argues, in this connection, that enforcement of the terms of the Ketubah by a civil court would violate the constitutional prohibition against excessive entanglement between church and State, because the court must necessarily intrude upon matters of religious doctrine and practice. It is urged that the obligations imposed by the Ketubah arise solely from Jewish religious law and can be interpreted only with reference to religious dogma. Granting the religious character of the Ketubah, it does not necessarily follow that any recognition of its obligations is foreclosed to the courts.

It is clear that judicial involvement in matters touching upon religious concerns has been constitutionally limited in analogous situations, and courts should not resolve such controversies in a manner requiring consideration of religious doctrine (*Presbyterian Church v Hull Church*, 393 US 440, 449; *Serbian Eastern Orthodox Diocese v Milivojevich*, 426 US 696, 709; *Jones v Wolf*, 443 US 595, 603; see e.g., *Reardon v Lemoyne*, ___ NH ___, ___ [Dec 23, 1982] In its most recent pronouncement on this issue, however, the Supreme Court, in holding that a State may adopt any approach to resolving religious disputes which does not entail consideration of doctrinal matters, specifically approved the use of the "neutral principles of law" approach as consistent with constitutional limitations (*Jones v Wolf, supra*, at p 602). This approach contemplates the application of objective, well-established principles of secular law to the dispute (*id.* at p 603), thus permitting judicial involvement to the extent that it can be accomplished in purely secular terms.

The present case can be decided solely upon the application of neutral principles of contract law, without reference to any religious principle. Consequently, defendant's objections to enforcement of his promise to appear before the Beth Din, based as they are upon the religious origin of the agreement, pose no constitutional barrier to the relief sought by plaintiff. The fact that the agreement was entered into as part of a religious ceremony does not render it unenforceable. Solemnization of the marital relationship often takes place in accordance with the religious beliefs of the participants, and this State has long recognized this religious aspect by permitting duly authorized pastors, rectors, priests, rabbis and other religious officials to perform the ceremony (Domestic Relations Law, § 11, subds 1, 7). Similarly, that the obligations undertaken by the parties to the Ketubah are grounded in religious belief and practice does not preclude enforcement of its secular terms. Nor does the fact that all of the Ketubah's provisions may not be judicially recognized prevent the court from enforcing that portion of the agreement by which the parties promised to refer their disputes to a nonjudicial forum (see *Ferro v Bologna*, 31 NY2d 30,36). The courts may properly enforce so much of this agreement as is not in contravention of law or public policy.

In short, the relief sought by plaintiff in this action is simply to compel defendant to perform a secular obligation to which he contractually bound himself. In this regard, no doctrinal issue need be passed upon, no implementation of a religious duty is contemplated, and no interference with religious authority will result. Certainly nothing the Beth Din can do would in any way affect the civil divorce. To the extent that an enforceable promise can be found by the application of neutral principles of contract law, plaintiff will have demonstrated entitlement to the relief sought. Consideration of other substantive issues bearing upon plaintiff's entitlement to a religious divorce, however, is appropriately left to the forum the parties chose for resolving the matter.

Accordingly, the order of the Appellate Division should be reversed, with costs, and defendant's motion to dismiss the complaint denied.

JONES, J. (dissenting):

We are of the opinion that to grant the relief plaintiff seeks in this action, even to the limited extent contemplated by the majority, would necessarily violate the constitutional prohibition against entanglement of our secular courts in matters of religious and ecclesiastical content. Accordingly, we would affirm the order of the Appellate Division.

We start on common ground. Judicial intervention in disputes with respect to religious and ecclesiastical obligation is constitutionally proscribed, save with respect to a narrow class of issues, as to which, under "neutral principles of law", the secular component of the religious and ecclesiastical rights and obligations may be resolved without impermissible trespass on or even reference to religious dogma and doctrine *** We depart from the conclusion of the majority that in this case the courts may discern one or more discretely secular obligations which may be fractured out of the "Ketubah", indisputably in its essence a document prepared and executed under Jewish law and tradition.

We are constrained, as is the majority, by the allegations of the complaint. Plaintiff therein alleges: that the parties were married on May 22, 1966 in a religious ceremony in accordance with Jewish law and tradition; that pursuant to the terms and conditions of the religious ceremony they entered into a contract known as a "Ketubah"; that under the Ketubah the husband declared and contracted with the wife to be her husband according to the law of Moses and Israel and to honor and support her, faithfully cherishing her and providing for her needs as Jewish husbands are required to do pursuant to Jewish religious law and tradition; that pursuant to the Ketubah the parties agreed to recognize the Beth Din of the Rabbinical Assembly and the Jewish Theological Seminary of America as having authority to summon either party at the request of the other and further agreed that in the event of any civil divorce decree the husband would grant and the wife accept a Jewish divorce ("get") in accordance with the authority vested in the Beth Din; that under the law of Moses should the husband arbitrarily refuse to give a "get" the wife, such as plaintiff in this case, is known and referred to as an "Aguna" which is a state of limbo wherein the wife is considered neither married nor divorced; that a judgment of civil divorce of the parties was entered on May 16, 1978 in the Albany County Clerk's Office; that the wife has requested and summoned the husband to appear before the Beth Din of the Rabbinical Assembly pursuant to the terms of the Ketubah but that he has willfully and intentionally refused to appear before the Assembly in violation of his contractual obligations; that in consequence the wife is consigned to the status of "Aguna" and is barred from remarrying within the context of a Jewish religious ceremony. The wife demands judgment against the husband: declaring "the rights and other legal relation of the plaintiff and defendant in the marriage contract (Ketubah), created by reason of the written instrument"; declaring that the husband specifically perform pursuant to the terms and conditions of the Ketubah in that he appear before the Beth Din of the Rabbinical Assembly and the Jewish Theological Seminary of America or its duly appointed representatives pursuant to the wife's request; declaring that failure of the husband so to appear constitutes a breach of contract; and for other incidental relief.

Determining whether judicial relief may be granted the wife without constitutionally impermissible interjection of the court into matters of religious and ecclesiastical content requres examination of the English translation of the Ketubah in the context of the wife's allegation that this document was made and entered into as part of the religious ceremony in accordance with Jewish law and tradition:

> On the *First* Day of the Week, the *3rd Day* of the Month *Sivan, 5726*, corresponding to the *22nd* Day of *May, 1966*, *Boaz Avitzur*, the bridegroom and *Susan Rose Wieder*, the bride, were united in marriage in *Old Westbury, N.Y.* The bridegroom made the following declaration to his bride: "Be thou my wife according to the law of Moses and Israel. I shall honor and support thee, faithfully I shall cherish thee and provide for thy needs, even as Jewish husbands are required to do by our religious law and tradition."
>
> In turn, the bride took upon herself the duties of a Jewish wife, to honor and cherish her husband, and to carry out all her obligations to him in faithfulness and affection as Jewish law and tradition prescribe.
>
> And in solemn assent to their mutual responsibilities and love, the bridegroom and bride have declared: As evidence of our desire to enable each other to live in accordance with the Jewish law of marriage throughout our lifetime, we, the bride and bridegroom, attach our signatures to this Ketubah, and hereby agree to recognize the

Beth Din of the Rabbinical Assembly and the Jewish Theological Seminary of America, or its duly appointed representatives, as having authority to counsel us in the light of Jewish tradition which requires husband and wife to give each other complete love and devotion, and to summon either party at the request of the other, in order to enable the party so requesting to live in accordance with the standards of the Jewish law of marriage throughout his or her lifetime.

We authorize the Beth Din to impose such terms of compensation as it may see fit for failure to respond to its summons or to carry out its decision.

This Ketubah was executed and witnessed this day in accordance with Jewish law and tradition.

Boaz Avitzur bridegroom *Susan Wieder* bride
Melvin Kieffer rabbi *Abraham Weisman* witness
Melvin Kieffer witness

At the outset we observe that the complaint contains no allegation that the parties intended that the Ketubah should manifest secular promises or have any civil or secular status or any legal significance independent of the religious ceremony between them of which it was an integral part. Nor is any such assertion advanced in the papers submitted by the wife in support of her cross motion for summary judgment.

Moreover, it appears evident to us that any determination of the content and particulars of the rights of the wife or the obligations of the husband under this document cannot be made without inquiry into and resolution of questions of Jewish religious law and tradition. We think it inaccurate to identify the relief sought by plaintiff, as does the majority, as "simply to compel defendant to perform a secular obligation to which he contractually bound himself" ***.

The complaint's first request for relief paints with a broad brush, asking that the court "declare the rights and other legal relation of the plaintiff and defendant in the marriage contract" created by reason of the Ketubah. That such an all-encompassing declaration of rights exceeds the authority of the civil court seems to be implicitly conceded by the majority's attempt to limit its consideration to enforcement of an obligation characterized as "secular" —the alleged obligation of the husband to appear before the Beth Din.

The wife's pleading itself, however, not to mention the affidavits submitted by her, makes it clear that even a definition of the purported "secular obligation" requires an examination into the principles and practice of the Jewish religion. Although the English translation of the Ketubah attached to the complaint recites that the parties "recognize the Beth Din *** as having authority *** to summon either party at the request of the other", the complaint seeks a declaration that the husband specifically perform "in that he appear before the Beth Din *** pursuant to the request of the plaintiff". Thus, the wife tenders her construction of the document, which in turn presumably is predicated on what she contends is tradition in the faith, i.e., that there is an obligation imposed by the agreement to appear before the Beth Din at the summons alone of the other party to the marriage despite the facial reference to a summons by the Beth Din. The husband, tendering his own construction of the document, denies that he is under any obligation to appear before the Beth Din because an earlier request by him for convocation of such a body was refused. Thus, it appears evident that any judicial determination whether the husband is obligated to appear before the Beth Din, or what nature of summons is required to call such obligation into play, necessarily involves reference to substantive religious and ecclesiastical law.*

The unsoundness of the position espoused by the majority to justify judicial action to compel the husband to appear before the Beth Din, is revealed by projection of the course the continuing litigation will take in this case. The motion to dismiss and the cross motion for summary judgment having both been denied, the case

---

*The recital in the testimonium clause itself is indicative—"this Ketubah was executed and witnessed this day in accordance with Jewish law and tradition."

will be set down for trial. The evidence which the wife may be expected to introduce is revealed by examination of the affidavits she submitted in opposition to the motion to dismiss and in support of her cross motion for summary judgment. Her affidavit conveys information furnished her by Rabbi Mordecai Kieffer who in his accompanying affidavit describes himself as "qualified to render an expert opinion concerning matters of Jewish laws and custom". She relies on his affidavit to support her claim that there was "good and legal consideration" for the Ketubah and that the Beth Din presently has no authority to compel the husband to submit to its jurisdiction. The Rabbi, predicated on what he offers as a more accurate translation of the Ketubah into English, expresses the opinion that "good and legal consideration" is to be found in the document itself. Then, describing in detail the procedures incident to the issuance of a "get", the Rabbi concludes that the husband was obligated to submit to the jurisdiction of the Beth Din without the issuance of any summons by it. Accordingly, it is evident that the wife and her counsel are themselves of the view that substantiation of her position will depend on expert opinion with respect to Jewish law and tradition.

The majority's reference to the fact that marriage relationships solemnized within a religious context are recognized by the civil law is not determinative of the question here presented where what is sought to be enforced is an aspect of the relationship peculiar to the religion within which the ceremony creating it took place. No authority is cited in which a civil court has enforced a concomitant undertaking required by the ecclesiastical authority under which the marriage ceremony was solemnized. That no such civil enforcement of the obligation to appear before the Beth Din was contemplated either by the drafter of the Ketubah or by the parties as its signatories is evident from the inclusion of explicit authorization to the Beth Din "to impose such terms of compensation as it may see fit for failure to respond to its summons or to carry out its decision". Nothing in the record suggests that it was the intention of the parties when they signed this religious document that the civil courts of the State of New York were to have jurisdiction to determine the substantive rights created thereby or to invoke civil procedures and remedies for the enforcement of such rights. Indeed, any conclusion on the part of our courts that this express provision was not intended by the parties as the exclusive remedy available to them for any breach of their obligations under the Ketubah would itself necessarily entail examination of Jewish law and tradition.

Finally, the evident objective of the present action—as recognized by the majority and irrefutably demonstrated by the complaint—even if procedural jurisdiction were to be assumed, is to obtain a religious divorce, a matter well beyond the authority of any civil court. (Again supplying her own interpretation of the Ketubah, the wife alleges: "That pursuant to the terms of the Ketubah, the plaintiff and defendant agreed that in the event of any civil divorce decree that the husband grant and the wife accept a Jewish divorce decree in accordance with the authority vested in the Beth Din of the Rabbinical Assembly".) As was noted at the Appellate Division, the interest of the civil authorities of the State of New York in the status of the marriage between these parties was concluded when the final judgment of divorce was entered in 1978.

Chief Judge COOKE and Judges FUCHSBERG and MEYER concur with Judge WACHTLER; Judge JONES dissents and votes to affirm in a separate opinion in which Judges JASEN and SIMONS concur.

Decided February 15, 1983.

GLOSSARY

AGUNAH, pl. *agunoth* (lit., a "chained woman"). A woman who is prevented from remarrying, either because of the disappearance of her husband, absent proof of his death, or because of his refusal to grant her a get.

AMATLA. A reasonable, adequate explanation or substantiation of a claim.

BETH DIN, pl. *battei din*. A duly constituted court of Jewish Law.

EIRUSIN. A marital status, conferring on the parties all the commitments and obligations of marriage with the exception of the right of cohabitation.

GEONIM, sing., *Gaon*. Heads of Rabbinic academies who flourished in Babylonia from approx. 600 C.E. to 1100 C.E.

GET, pl. *gittin*. A bill of divorce. Also, the divorce proceedings.

ḤALITZAH (lit., "removal of the shoe"). The ceremony which releases a childless widow from the obligation to marry the brother of her deceased husband.

ḤEREM. Excommunication, as in "Ḥerem of Rabbenu Gershom," applied against any man who divorces his wife against her will, or who enters into a bigamous marriage.

KETUBAH. The marriage contract presented to the bride by the groom in which are enumerated all of the husbandly obligations.

KIDDUSHIN. (lit., "consecration"). The legal act of marriage which may be carried out in one of three ways: by the groom's presentation of an object of value to the bride, by formal writ, or by cohabitation. Nowadays, the first-mentioned is practiced exclusively.

KINYAN. A formal act of acquisition.

KOHEN, pl. *Kohanim*. Of priestly stock: descendant of Aaron, brother of Moses.

MAMZER, pl. *mamzerim*. A bastard: offspring of an adulterous union.

MA'US ALAY (lit., "He is repulsive to me"). A woman's claim that her husband is repulsive to her which, according to some authorities, is sufficient cause for her to be granted a divorce.

MISHNAH. A definitive collection of Jewish law, prepared and edited by Rabbi Yehuda Hanasi, in approximately 220 C.E. Rabbis of the Mishnaic period are known as *Tannaim*.

MOREDET. A rebellious wife is considered to be a moredet if she knowingly violates Torah law or conventional morality, or if she refuses to engage in sexual relations with her husband.

NISUIN. The consummation of the marriage.

SHTAR. A formal writ or document.

SHULHAN ARUKH (lit., "Prepared Table"). The authoritative Code of Jewish Law, compiled in the 16th century by Rabbi Yosef Karo.

TAKANAH, pl., *takanot*. An authoritative legislative decree, enacted by duly constituted Rabbinic authorities.

TALMUD. The Oral Law. The Talmud consists of the Mishnah and the Gemara. The Gemara was completed at about 500 C.E. The Rabbis of the Gemara, who flourished between 220 C.E. and 500 C.E., are called *Amoraim*.